ROOSEVELT
AND
STALIN

ROOSEVELT AND STALIN

The Failed Courtship

BY

ROBERT NISBET

REGNERY GATEWAY
Washington, D.C.

Library of Congress Cataloging-in-Publication Data

Nisbet, Robert A.
    Roosevelt and Stalin : the failed courtship / by Robert Nisbet.
        p.   cm.
    Includes index.
    ISBN 0-89526-558-3 : $14.95
    1. Roosevelt, Franklin D. (Franklin Delano), 1882–1945.
    2. Stalin, Joseph, 1879–1953.   3. World War, 1939–1945—
United States.   4. World War, 1939–1945—Soviet Union.   5. World War,
1939–1945—Diplomatic history.   I. Title.
E807.N55   1988
973.917′092′4—dc19   88-22061
                                                                 CIP

Published by Regnery Gateway
1130 17th Street, NW, Washington, DC 20036

Distributed to the trade by Kampmann & Company, Inc.
9 E. 40th Street, New York, NY 10016

Manufactured in the United States of America

Designed by Irving Perkins Associates

10 9 8 7 6 5 4 3 2 1

ACKNOWLEDGMENTS

This book is the outgrowth of an article on Roosevelt's courtship of Stalin for *Modern Age* (Spring 1986 and Summer/Fall 1986) at the invitation of its editor, Dr. George A. Panichas. I take pleasure in thanking Dr. Panichas publicly for the stimulus he provided to what proved to be a couple of years of engrossing reading and writing. I thank also Henry Regnery, exemplary publisher and humane mind, for his encouragement of the book. Once again I record my indebtedness to my wife for her unique role in this as in other books.

CONTENTS

ROOSEVELT
AND
STALIN

INTRODUCTION

It is unlikely that history holds a stranger, more improbable, and withal consequential relationship than that between President Roosevelt and Marshal Stalin in World War II. It was more of a courtship than a relationship in the ordinary sense; a courtship initiated by the President and regarded warily by the Marshal throughout, almost as though he could scarcely credit what was before his eyes.

The very idea of the courtship is arresting: Roosevelt, patrician, born with a silver spoon, Groton- and Harvard-educated, aristocrat in American politics, deeply devoted to his national heritage; Stalin, low-born, bandit and revolutionist from his early years, successor by sheer ruthlessness to Lenin as absolute ruler of Russia, liquidator of millions of Ukrainians, cruel purger of his own party in the Moscow Trials of the mid-1930s, executioner of untold numbers of Spanish socialists during the Civil War in which he was purportedly their ally, eager participant with Hitler in the dismemberment of Poland and the Baltic States in 1939, and totalitarian to the core.

3

Roosevelt's pursuit of Stalin during World War II is well known, thanks to four decades of memoirs, official documents, and intensive war-studies. But it is certainly *not* well understood or well remembered, if the recent work of journalists and historians is anything to go by. In the minds of some Americans, even to refer to Roosevelt's efforts to charm and capture Stalin for democracy is to verge on McCarthyism. This is unfortunate. For however history finally assesses Roosevelt's part in the Roosevelt-Stalin relationship—as one of high-minded idealism and concern for postwar peace and democracy or as a compound of Roosevelt's political romanticism, credulity, and personal arrogance—it is pointless and futile to deny or hide the relationship itself.

It is not as though, for our consideration of the Roosevelt courtship, we were obliged to go to prejudiced sources, ambiguous documents, and hearsay. Far from it. The courtship was visible to many at the top in the war, and it was noted and commented on, in one context or other, by persons deeply loyal and faithful to the President to the very end.

His Secretary of Labor, Frances Perkins, was one of these. In her book, *The Roosevelt I Knew,* she recounts a conversation she had in the White House with FDR just after his return from a meeting with the Soviet leaders. He was plainly impressed by the Russians, and Secretary Perkins mentioned that someone she had talked with spoke of the Russian people's "desire to do the Holy Will." To which the President replied: "You know, there may be something in that. It would explain their almost mystical devotion to this idea which they have developed of the Communist society. They all seem really to want to do what is good for their society instead of wanting to do for themselves. We take care of ourselves and think about the welfare of society afterward."[1]

In the same conversation, Roosevelt averred that while he knew the difference between a "good" and a "bad" Frenchman, he wasn't sure he knew a good Russian from a bad one. Would Miss Perkins therefore keep her eyes open in her reading and let him know if she found anything pertinent? Of course FDR could have gone to such profoundly informed advisers as Loy Henderson, Charles E. "Chip" Bohlen, or George Kennan for help, but that would have violated his strict avoidance of all experts.

Averell Harriman, close friend, adviser, and faithful envoy to the President, has written that Roosevelt was a "forerunner" to the "convergence school." He believed:

[H]is New Deal Revolution had expanded American ideas about the government's social responsibility. . . . In the Soviets he saw the completely centralized state bureaucracy giving way to a degree of decentralization. . . .

He was determined, establishing a close personal relationship with Stalin in wartime, to build confidence among the Kremlin leaders that Russia, now an acknowledged major power, could trust the West.

For my part, although I did not disagree with his basic approach, I was far less optimistic in the time it would take. I also believed it would be far more difficult than Roosevelt imagined to develop a real basis of mutual confidence with Stalin. . . .

Churchill had a more pragmatic attitude. He too would have liked to build on wartime intimacy to achieve postwar understandings. But his mind concentrated on the settlement of specific political problems and spheres of influence. He despised Communism and all its works. He turned pessimistic about the future earlier than Roosevelt. And he foresaw much greater difficulties at the end of the war.[2]

To the best of our knowledge, Roosevelt always remained confident of his courtship of Stalin. There are some historians who claim to find a significant change in Roosevelt's attitude toward Stalin shortly before Roosevelt's death. Roosevelt expressed irritation or disillusionment a couple of times during the post-Yalta spring of 1945 when Stalin was crudely and rampantly violating his Yalta promises in eastern Europe. Perhaps so. But in Roosevelt's correspondence with Churchill and Stalin there is no sign of such a negative reaction. We have Harriman's judgment of the matter: "There is no persuasive evidence that he was disposed to abandon his efforts at winning Stalin's cooperation."[3]

George Kennan was also aware of the President's efforts to win Stalin's favor and to bring the dictator's mind within a democratic and liberal pale. After a general indictment of Allied embassy staffs for their ignorance compounded with self-deception, Kennan turns to Roosevelt himself.

I also have in mind FDR's evident conviction that Stalin, while perhaps a somewhat difficult customer, was only, after all, a person like any other person; that the reason we hadn't been able to get along with him in the past was that we had never really had anyone with the proper personality and the proper qualities of sympathy and imagination to deal with him . . . and that if only he could be exposed to the persuasive charms of someone like FDR himself, ideological preconceptions would melt and Stalin's cooperation with the West could easily be arranged. For these assumptions there were no grounds whatsoever; and they were of a puerility unworthy of a statesman of FDR's stature.[4]

William Bullitt was concerned throughout the war with what he believed was Roosevelt's indulgent attitude toward Stalin and the Soviets and his indifference to their well known record of military aggressiveness and cruel despotism. Bullitt was a long-time friend of the President's. He was sent by FDR as America's first ambassador to the Soviet Union in the early 1930s, after official American recognition of the Soviets commenced under the President. During the war he was an unofficial adviser at the White House, and spent a considerable amount of time trying, without success, to stiffen Roosevelt's stance in Soviet matters. In January 1943, Bullitt put together a long letter to his chief, one that George Kennan later referred to as "among the major historical documents of the time . . . unique in the insights it brought." The gist of it was Bullitt's plea to the President to use toward Stalin "the old technique of the donkey, carrot, and club." Beyond that, however, the letter was a matchless treatise on Soviet geopolitics, diplomatic and military history, and highly probable annexations of eastern European countries after the war.[5]

Once when Bullitt urged the President to be less liberal with Stalin in such matters as lend-lease, Roosevelt replied: "I think if I give him everything I possibly can, and ask nothing from him in return, *noblesse oblige,* he won't try to annex anything and will work with me for a world of peace and democracy."[6]

Not much light is shed on the Stalin-Roosevelt relationship in Churchill's great history of the Second World War. All the volumes are profoundly expressive of the main currents of the war and of the war's intimacies and antagonisms at a high level. It deserved the Nobel Prize in Literature it received. But there is almost nothing about Roosevelt's relationship with Stalin and the several serious problems this relationship presented during the war for Churchill and his British military advisers: problems of tactics, strategy, and policy in the war. The reason for this reticence is given in a letter Churchill wrote President Eisenhower in 1953 just as the final volume of his history was due to appear:

I am most anxious that nothing should be published which might seem to others to threaten our current relations in our public duties or impair the sympathy and understanding which existed between our two countries. I have therefore gone over the book again in the last few months and have taken great pains to ensure that it contains nothing which might imply that there was any controversy or lack of confidence between us. There was in fact little controversy in those years; but I have been careful to ensure that the few differences of opinion which arose are so described that even ill-disposed people will be unable to turn them to mischievous account.[7]

This is an astonishing letter in what it reveals of Churchill's mind and his disposition toward pragmatic adjustment at whatever cost to the truth. For, as will become evident enough in successive chapters, there were some major controversies between Roosevelt and Churchill during the war, controversies duly noted by Churchill himself, sometimes passionately, other times in manifest sorrow. Nearly all of them had to do with Churchill's and his military staff's recognition not later than the Teheran summit meeting at the end of 1943 that a very special and, to Churchill, deeply troubling relationship between the President and Stalin was emerging.

We may honor Churchill's motives in the letter he wrote to President Eisenhower in 1953. He sincerely and properly didn't want to muddy American waters; he was eager to maintain warm relations between himself and Eisenhower; he very much wanted his cherished dream of an Anglo-American Union to come to fruition. But the fact remains: His letter to Ike indicates that the full truth was by no means the only criterion Churchill went by as he readied the final volume of his war memoirs for publication. I should add that Churchill was in his second term as Prime Minister when he wrote to Eisenhower.

It is this Churchillian reticence or delicacy in occasional matters having to do with the Americans in the war that gives Martin Gilbert's volume, *Winston S. Churchill: Road to Victory: 1941–1945,* extra value. In its densely packed pages, based upon access to every known document pertaining to Churchill's life and career, a great deal more of the truth, the reality, of the Roosevelt-Stalin relationship emerges, as do reactions on Churchill's part of censure, anguish, and disappointment. I have made much use of this invaluable work.

So have I of the *Complete Correspondence* which was conducted secretly by Roosevelt and Churchill from the time Roosevelt initiated it on September 11, 1939, until the President's death on April 12, 1945. Superbly edited by Professor Warren Kimball of Rutgers University, the three large volumes form a treasure trove of the Second World War. For years, these letters with their riches lay under secrecy regulations adopted during the war, and it was not until Princeton University Press, after all secrecy had been removed from the complete collection, published them in 1984, in a sterling act of public service, that the world was allowed in their rich contents. Any reader's first reaction to the two thousand communications, covering nearly six years of war, is one of astonishment that two war leaders could have maintained the high level of civility, of warmth, and of mutual courtesy that are to be found in their voluminous correspondence with each other.

Courtesy and warmth notwithstanding, there were genuine strains and tensions between the two men over the terrible loss of lives and ships in the convoys to northern Russia; over the timing of the cross-Channel second front that Stalin incessantly urged in the Russian interest in the east; over the gift by FDR of a third of the Italian fleet to the Soviets; over the Warsaw Uprising and Allied obligations regarding it; over the Soviet violations in the spring of 1945 of the Yalta agreements (and other delinquencies of the Russians); and—to Churchill the most anguishing of all the issues that divided the two men—over the refusal of Roosevelt and his chief advisers, starting with General Marshall, to cooperate in a Mediterranean strategy that would have made Anglo-American penetration of the "soft underbelly" of Nazi-held Europe as prominent as the strategy of head-on conflict across the Channel. Churchill regarded the Mediterranean strategy not only as a means to cripple the German war effort, but, by virtue of the Anglo-American presence, also to guard against Soviet domination of central and eastern Europe after the war. Finally, there are letters in the collection that throw some light on Eisenhower's highly controversial decision, made strictly on his own authority, to bypass Berlin, leaving its momentous conquest entirely to the Soviets, in the final weeks of the war.

Two things are important to keep in mind. The first is that after 1942, as the American arsenal began to reach its astonishing yield of materiel and troops in western Europe, Roosevelt had the power that went with American riches, and Churchill knew this only too well. The second is the artfulness, almost from the beginning, of Churchill's designs on Roosevelt. Sir John Colville describes a small dinner with Churchill late in the war, at which Churchill acknowledged the vital, the key, role of Roosevelt and American power and the necessity from the beginning of dealing with the President with the utmost tact and favor, no matter how far apart they might be on such policy matters as the proper time for a cross-Channel assault. "No lover," said Churchill, "ever studied every whim of his mistress as I did those of President Roosevelt."[8]

Only once in the long correspondence did Churchill show himself to Roosevelt as angry about American actions and at the same time resentful of partiality toward Stalin and the Soviets. The State Department, under Edward Stettinius, issued, without prior notice to the British government, a White Paper that excoriated Great Britain for certain ventures in Italy and Greece which, the White Paper charged, revealed both British imperialism and political reaction.

Churchill, stung by the State Department's public censure of an ally, wrote on December 6, 1944, to Roosevelt: "I do not remember anything that the State Department has ever said about Russia comparable to this document. . . . I am sure such things have never been said by the State Department about Russia even when very harsh communications have been received and harsher deeds done."

Churchill recognized fully the necessity of doing business with Stalin and keeping him reasonably happy. Sad to say, he could join Roosevelt in fulsome toasts at banquets at Teheran and Yalta, toasts to Stalin himself and to the Soviet Union and all its works. Even the fact of Roosevelt's deliberate exclusion of Churchill from the confidential talks the President had arranged with Stalin behind Churchill's back didn't interfere with the Prime Minister's unmitigated public approval of his two indispensable allies. When Stalin was dragged into war in June 1941 by the German invasion, Churchill welcomed Stalin in words that might have been addressed to a Pericles or George Washington. Before the whole world, Churchill greeted the Soviets as fellow freedom fighters protecting their own liberties and democracy. Reading it today, one becomes slightly nauseated by Churchill's words and Roosevelt's own concurring greetings. It was one thing to make the best of things, to accept and even help Stalin in the war against the Nazis, and to see clearly the very real aid that would come from the Russian-German war in the East, while the western Allies were engaging Hitler across the Channel. It was something else, and hardly necessary, given Stalin's then desperate straits, to lavish gratitude upon the cruel, terror-minded despot who, after all, had helped ignite World War II against the West. But when all this embarrassing schmooze is revealed, with even Churchill's acquiescence in the odious Declaration on Liberated Europe at Yalta kept firmly in mind, there is still evident in Churchill, throughout his career following the First World War, a distrust and fear of Communism and of the Soviet Union that Roosevelt never shared. Churchill let up on condemnation of the Soviet Union only when, in 1933, he saw the immediately greater menace of Hitler to

Europe and the world. Even so, as late as 1939, Churchill accepted an invitation to write a book on the impact of Communist Russia on Europe. Throughout the war there were, as we shall see, remarks made and minutes dispatched to some of those close to him, such as Anthony Eden, Alan Brooke, and Lord Moran, that made evident his persisting distrust of the Soviets in the postwar world.

There is no evidence of any analogous feeling on Roosevelt's part. Once Roosevelt criticized the Soviets publicly during the period of the Soviet-Nazi Pact. He was addressing a Communist-led American student association, at the request of his wife, and the booing of him was immediate. It may have been the only time in his life he was booed by an audience. Late in the war, Roosevelt wrote angrily to Stalin, on his own and Churchill's behalf, after Stalin had written them a very harsh letter accusing them (baselessly) of negotiating a separate peace with the Nazis. But, as subsequent correspondence indicated, the President got over his anger quickly.

For whatever reasons, the attitude of the White House toward the Soviets was benign from the beginning of Roosevelt's presidency. Secretary Cordell Hull in his memoirs wrote, with exasperation and some disgust, of the ease with which the Soviets were given recognition early in the New Deal. Little if any attention was paid to rules and prohibitions affecting the Soviet embassy and its consulates across the country, in which Soviet spies and other agents abounded. Although the FBI was instructed to give the closest scrutiny to possible German agents and also to the comical German-American Bund in New York, there appears to have been no such interest in the White House during the 1930s in Soviet espionage. When Whittaker Chambers brought the account of his, the Hisses's, and others's underground work for the Communist Party to Adolf Berle at the State Department in 1939, nothing followed. Berle merely put his notes on Chambers's devastating testimony in a private file. The truth is, throughout the New Deal and World War II, any accusations of either Communist or Soviet underground participation yielded an immediate chorus of "red baiting" from most liberals.

Two incidents nicely illustrate the differences between the Prime Minister and the President in their respective attitudes toward Stalin and the Soviets. At one point in the war, Eden asked Churchill for his precise and confidential views on the postwar relationship between Russia and the rest of the European continent. Churchill wrote: "It would be a measureless disaster if Russian barbarism overlaid the ancient states of Europe." What he hoped for, he added, was a "United States of Europe," one specifically excluding the Soviet Union, in which "the barriers between nations will be greatly minimized and unrestricted travel will be possible," guarded, however, by an international police force one of whose tasks would be "keeping Russia disarmed."[9]

At about the same time, Roosevelt had a serious conversation with Francis Cardinal Spellman of New York on the probable shape of postwar Europe. The President said that the European people—not just the eastern European, note, but the *European* people—would simply have to "endure Russian domination in the hope that—in ten or twenty years—the European influence would bring the Russians to become less barbarous."[10] At the First Quebec Conference, Churchill told an intimate that he saw "bloody consequences in the future" coming out of Soviet war strength. He added: "Stalin is an unnatural man." "There will be grave troubles."[11] There is not one comment or fragment of a comment in Roosevelt's entire career, down to his death on April 12, 1945, when the Soviets had been for many weeks smashing their Yalta promises in eastern Europe, to suggest an analogous sentiment on Roosevelt's part.

In his credulity toward Stalin and the real nature of Russian Communism, Roosevelt was not, of course, alone in America. In academic, journalistic, entertainment, and other circles there was wide-eyed adulation of Stalin after the Nazis invaded Russia in June 1941. Even after VE Day such respected journalists as Walter Lippman and Raymond Gram Swing literally walked out of a Harriman briefing on Soviet realities. And weeks later, after the notable Westminster College "iron curtain" speech, Churchill came in for considerable criticism in the United States, from major newspapers, the churches, colleges and universities, and others. Even Truman, who had invited Churchill to be the speaker and whose attitude toward Stalin and the Soviets was measurably more severe than Roosevelt's had been, was somewhat unhappy, we are told.

The fact is, a large number of Americans had become, as the war went on and as the Soviet armies fought back the invading Germans, more and more friendly to godless Russia. Some of this, as we shall see, was Roosevelt's doing. He fought hard in late 1941 to offset, to root out, American—especially religious—dislike of the Soviets. The attitude toward Soviets throughout the war from the White House, State Department, and War Department was scrupulously uncritical—as an aggrieved Winston Churchill observed in one of his letters to the President—but far from uncritical about the British, as the American response to Britain's Christmas 1944 rescue of Greece from the Communist forces proved. It never occurred to Roosevelt to see the structure of Soviet society as being close to that of Nazi Germany, as, in other words, totalitarian in both cases. It did to Churchill.

Churchill had at least some notion of what the totalitarian state was, could see that whether in Communist, Fascist, or Nazi form, its founders, and its ideological message, were essentially socialist, and that to call either Fascist Italy or Nazi Germany a form of capitalism was nonsense. Roosevelt saw in Stalin's Russia, equality, social justice, and social democracy growing underneath the top dressing of force necessary to repulse capitalists and other enemies of the Soviet Union. Churchill was shrewd enough to know that Stalin's Russia was despotism to the very core, resting on terror and incessant indoctrination beneath the lulling rhetoric of egalitarianism.

But to impute to Roosevelt, as some did during the McCarthy era, disloyalty or lack of patriotism, is absurd. The distinguished British diplomatic historian, A. J. P. Taylor, has argued that of the Big Three, it was Roosevelt who got the most for his country out of the war; even more than Stalin in eastern Europe and in Asia. Taylor was referring to such American economic gains as civil air routes throughout the world, favorable tariff concessions, monetary stabilization to American advantage, and so on. He may have also had in mind the unprecedented and unequalled prosperity that the United States has known since World War II. Some of these gains were the products of the private war FDR conducted on British and French imperialism during the war against Nazi Germany.

But although no reasonable challenges to the President's patriotism and loyalty to American ideals can be made, it doesn't follow that Roosevelt is without guilt in other respects affecting the Soviet Union. As the pages following will make evident enough, Roosevelt played the credulous ape throughout the war as far as Stalin and the Soviets were concerned. If it is said that there was no alternative or that he was insufficiently advised and alerted by his war aides, the answer is, "Nonsense." Three ambassadors, William Bullitt, Admiral Standley, and Averell Harriman tried to warn him; so did such Russian experts as George Kennan, Loy Henderson, and Charles Bohlen. To no avail. At Teheran, FDR played essentially the role Chamberlain had at Munich. Stalin was no more averse than Hitler to the cruel pleasure of smiting bearers of gifts. The practice has long been the sport of despots.

That Roosevelt had valuable qualities as president during both the Depression and the Second World War goes without saying. Many journalists and historians have highlighted these qualities and snapped at any writer who has seen warts here and there. Rarely has any American president—certainly not Washington or Lincoln—enjoyed the press acclaim during a war that Roosevelt did during the Second World War. By dint of the great Arsenal of Democracy, American productive genius kept much Russian and British as well as American war momentum going. It is questionable whether either the Soviets or the British, or both, could have defeated Hitler without the waves of American materiel and manpower crossing the Atlantic.

But it has to be, and should be, recorded that along with virtues and excellences in his leadership there was one gigantic failure, one that postwar history has steadily magnified in seriousness: the failure to recognize the obvious in Stalin and the Soviet Union or even to listen to those of his own country who did recognize the obvious and tried repeatedly to convey it to the President's attention, as Ambassadors Bullitt, Standley, and Harriman, among others did, but without the slightest success.

Aides and associates of the President like Harriman, Kennan, Bohlen, Bullitt, Loy Henderson, and Joseph Grew may have disagreed among themselves on some issues pertaining to the Soviet Union—on, for example, the degree to which the aggressiveness and domestic terrorism of Stalinist Russia was better explained as an ingrained *Russian* trait, with Marxism-Leninism little more than an ideological fig-leaf, or as a *Communist* trait born of a Marxist hatred of capitalism and the bourgeoisie. But on one point, these men were agreed: The Soviet Union was not a fit ally for the United States and was America's most dangerous enemy in the postwar world.

There is no evidence that Roosevelt gave more than the most cursory attention to the views of these men, all of them deeply experienced in Russian and world affairs, all of them impeccably devoted to the United States and, for that matter, to the Roosevelt war administration. He seems to have preferred the counsel on Russian matters of Harry Hopkins, Joseph Davies, Admiral Leahy, General Marshall, his Secretary of Labor Frances Perkins, and other amateurs.

It was only after Roosevelt's death and Truman's accession to the White House that men like Harriman, Kennan, and Bohlen—who were effectively joined by such like-minded wartime officials as James Forrestal,

John McCloy, Robert Lovett, and Joseph Grew—were able to issue warnings about Stalin and the Soviets that the White House took seriously. It may be said that by the fall of 1945 the depredations of the Soviets upon eastern Europe were so obvious and so revolting that any president, possibly FDR himself, would have seen what the Soviets were up to and taken necessary action. That, however, is unlikely, to say the least. Churchill and Harriman had rained reports and warnings on Roosevelt during the weeks between Yalta and his death in April 1945. He was seemingly impervious to their advice. Why would he have been different at the end of 1945?

Perhaps Roosevelt, had he lived into the early months of 1946, would have conceded at last the validity of the warnings of Bullitt, Harriman, Churchill, Kennan, and Bohlen. For on February 9, speaking to the Soviet people from the Bolshoi Theatre in Moscow, Stalin savagely attacked the capitalist world, and in so doing specifically included the United States and Britain in that world. Contradictions in capitalism had caused the Second World War, Stalin said, and the same contradictions in the United States and western Europe were already threatening to cause a third world war. The speech brought an immediate and serious verbal reaction from the Truman White House; whether it would have had in Roosevelt's is not at all certain.

Karl Marx, echoing Hegel's belief that great events in history tend to repeat themselves, added: "The first time as tragedy; the second time as farce." In the First World War Woodrow Wilson's career ended in tragedy: the defeat of his cherished League of Nations by the Senate. There was tragedy in Roosevelt's end too: the rape of Poland by Stalin's Red Army during the last two months Roosevelt was alive. But within the tragedy lay a farce: the farce of a war-long belief held by Roosevelt that he could convert the bestial Stalin into something on the order of a Bronx Democrat.

CHAPTER
ONE

"I Can Personally Handle Stalin"

On March 18, 1942, a bare three months after America's entry into the war, Roosevelt wrote these words in a letter to Churchill:

> I know you will not mind my being brutally frank when I tell you that I think I can personally handle Stalin better than either your Foreign Office or my State Department. Stalin hates the guts of all your top people. He thinks he likes me better, and I hope he will continue to.[1]

What could possibly have led the President to write those words to Churchill, which the Prime Minister entered in his war memoirs but without comment? Roosevelt had never met Stalin and knew almost nothing about Soviet affairs except what he had been told by his ambassadors to Russia, from William Bullitt through Joseph Davies down to the current incumbent, Admiral Standley. FDR had disliked Bullitt's generally critical reports on the Soviets, and had transferred Bullitt to France where he stayed until France was occupied by Germany in 1940. The

15

ambassador Roosevelt *did* like was Joseph Davies, a diplomat-business-man and ardent admirer of the Soviets. Within weeks after his arrival at the American embassy in Moscow in 1937, the embassy's able and experienced professional diplomatic staff, then working under the acting direction of Loy Henderson and George Kennan, actually held a meeting, in private, to consider a group resignation to protest Davies's rank ama-teurishness and invincible ignorance of Soviet history and Soviet barbar-ism. They chose to endure Davies for the year or two they knew he planned to hold the ambassadorship, but no longer.

When Davies and his wealthy wife returned to the U.S. after spending about a year in Moscow and a little more than a year in Belgium, it was to write his notorious *Mission to Moscow*—impolitely referred to by the Kennan group as *Submission to Moscow*—an unapologetic, uncrit-ical paean of praise to the Soviets. The book was published in 1941 when Roosevelt was working overtime to build up favorable sentiment for the Soviets in the United States, and was an immediate hit. The movie was an even bigger hit, and from it an American movie audience could have logically concluded that the Soviet leaders were all Abraham Lincolns.

George Kennan's *Memoirs* throws an interesting light on the strongly pro-Soviet disposition of the White House. Beginning in 1924, there was a small Division of Eastern European Affairs in the State Department under the directorship of the brilliant and scholarly Robert F. Kelley, who was anything but an admirer of the Soviets. According to Kennan, the division had the best library in the United States on Soviet history, and included "elaborate and voluminous files of materials collected from every possible source on every aspect of Soviet life." Even Litvinov paid the division a high if bitter compliment when he said that nothing as complete and ordered existed in Moscow.

Kennan writes that "some five months after Davies' entry upon his duties as ambassador," Kelley was suddenly ordered by the under secre-tary of state to break up the Russian division and scatter its precious holdings.

> The beautiful library was to be turned over to the Library of Congress, to be dispersed there by file numbers among its vast holdings. . . . The special files were to be destroyed. The division was to be reduced to two desks in the new European Divisions.
>
> I never learned the real background for this curious purge. . . . There is strong evidence that pressure was brought to bear from the White House. I

was surprised, in later years, that the McCarthyites and other right-wingers of the early Fifties never got hold of the incident and made capital of it, for here, if ever, was a point at which there was indeed the smell of Soviet influence, or strongly pro-Soviet influence somewhere in the higher reaches of the government.

The Russian Division, in any case, was abolished—with a suddenness more characteristic of Soviet politics than of American administrative procedure. Kelley was packed off to the embassy at Ankara and retired from the service a few years later.[2]

The only cheerful note in this, and it is minute relatively, is that Kennan, just returning to the United States, learned instantly of the action and, with the help of his friend Bohlen, managed to rescue several hundred of the most valuable reference books and to conceal them first in the attic of the State Department and then restore them to book cases in their offices.

It is very hard to imagine that so important a move as this one in the Department organization, wiping out a division, and so harsh a disposal of very valuable books and documents could have occurred without specific instruction—in whatever style or manner—from the White House. Davies, fresh in his ambassadorship in Moscow, knowing only too well his unpopularity with his staff of experts at the embassy and eager to impress Stalin and the Soviet leaders, may have specifically requested it of the President in a confidential dispatch. But irrespective of the details, the appointment of Davies coincided with, indeed resulted from, a feeling in the White House and among liberals generally in the country that the relationship between Moscow and Washington should become closer and warmer, that America should realize that her most natural ally in the world was the Soviet Union, which, it was argued, with all its warts, was still closer to true democracy than were the imperialist states of Britain, France, and, of course, the unspeakable Italy and Germany.

By the late 1930s, the White House was unapologetically friendly toward the USSR, though the State Department, for the most part, was not. Charles Bohlen says that when he first met Harry Hopkins at the White House, Hopkins "rudely" asked him if he "was a part of the anti-Soviet clique at the State Department." Bohlen chose to remain tactful with the powerful Hopkins.[3]

The Hitler-Stalin Pact of August 1939 was a jolt to the White House and the liberal mind in America. But it was entirely acceptable to Stalin and Molotov, who worked constantly between 1939 and 1941 to make the

Russo-German agreement into an actual war alliance. It was to no avail. Hitler simply bided his time, striking Russia on June 22, 1941, just as British Intelligence had futilely warned Moscow he would.[4]

The Pact embarrassed American Communists and fellow-travellers, but they loyally defended the alliance of Russia with Hitler's Germany, declaring World War II a purely imperialistic war that America should stay out of. Pro-Soviet forces in the U.S. cheered the war, however, the moment Hitler's armies invaded Russia. Isolation and America First were buried instantly to be replaced by "Second Front Now" banners everywhere.

A large and solid body of religious opinion, with Roman Catholics in the front, disliked Stalin's godless Russia and its constitutional prohibition of religious worship at least as much as it disliked Nazi Germany, where at least some forms of religion were left standing. This mattered a great deal to the White House's efforts to supply the Soviets with lend-lease and other aid. Given their strongly religious constituents, many congressmen were far from eager to cooperate with the administration. Why, it was repeatedly asked, ally ourselves with a totalitarian state like Russia in the war in Europe?

Clearly, if help in large quantities was to be provided the Soviets, something had to be done at home to counteract the image of a godless, religion-hating Soviet Union. Something also had to be done to counteract the widespread conviction that Germany would easily defeat Russia, even before Christmas, given the speed with which the Germans were advancing eastward.

The really overwhelming fact, though, that the White House and all pro-Soviet forces in the U.S. had to cope with was that Russia's entrance into the war as a *de facto* ally of Britain and the United States greatly changed the character of the war. The war could no longer be called one of "democracy vs. totalitarianism." For in all particulars Soviet Russia was at very least as totalitarian as Hitler's Germany. George Kennan has recorded his own immediate appreciation of this fundamental change in the character of the war. He was then in the American embassy in Berlin. When the word came of the German invasion of Russia, Kennan wrote immediately to the Russian Division of the State Department, saying that while collaboration between America and the Soviets would be necessary, he did "want to voice the hope that never would we associate ourselves with Russian purposes in the areas of eastern Europe beyond her own borders."[5]

Kennan's wisdom didn't have a chance. Not only Roosevelt, but even Churchill wanted only to greet the Soviets ecstatically as the new member of the Grand Alliance, or United Nations, as the partnership between the U.S. and Britain was known. On the very day, Kennan writes, that he penned his note to the State Department, the Prime Minister had already prepared remarks of welcome to the Soviets that would include: "The Russian danger is . . . our danger, and the danger of the United States, just as the cause of any Russian fighting for his hearth and home is the cause of the free men and free people in every quarter of the globe."[6]

To this Roosevelt gave his full support.

It may be said that we have no right today to judge such a statement, such a gross caricature of reality, by the criteria of hindsight. But there were a great many Americans and British then, in June 1941, who questioned sharply the words used and the spirit which prevailed with respect to Stalin and his country. Once he had come out of his self-imposed isolation of shock at his betrayal by Hitler, Stalin was shouting to the world, through his highly aggressive ambassadors in London and Washington, that it was the duty of Great Britain and the United States to come immediately to his assistance: Stalin who had had almost equal effect with Hitler in starting the War on the West in 1939; Stalin who in 1939 after the war had begun, declared in *Pravda* that "It is not Germany who has attacked England and France, but England and France who have attacked Germany."

Not once did Churchill and Roosevelt make it plain to Stalin that although the two Allies were, in the common interest of the war, entirely willing to provide such help as they could, they were not acquiescing in or subscribing to the territorial gains the Soviets had made in the pact with Hitler.

As Kennan points out, there was something to be said for Churchill's open-armed welcome. After all, in June 1941 America was still short of actual participation in the war, and Churchill had known ever since the fall of France in 1940 the terrible isolation and ever-present danger of being alone in the war against Nazi Germany. But for Roosevelt in June 1941, when America was not yet in the fighting and had only the most dubious prospects for getting in, there was no real excuse for his ebullient welcome of Communist Russia to the "common cause of all free men." There was not so much as a condition laid down, not a warning that in return for the lend-lease aid about to be so generously distributed to the

Soviets, Stalin would be held to stiff accounting after the war with respect to his territorial gains under the Pact.

The ever-cited reason for Stalin not having been pressed, is that Russia might have, in vengeful anger, dropped out of the war against Hitler, perhaps through some arranged peace, thus depriving Britain and America of an eastern front against the Nazis. Perhaps there was that danger, though I doubt it. Just as Stalin unfailingly responded to kindness from the West with a snarl, so, almost equally unfailingly, he was at his most agreeable when confronted by sternness, especially in respect to badly needed materiel from America and Britain. In apparently abject fright on June 22, and during the days afterward, he almost decided, from the deep of his self-prescribed isolation in the Kremlin, to move the Soviet government several hundred miles to the east where Hitler's forces would not be sent, surrendering Moscow, Leningrad, and the rest of western Russia. But by the time Hopkins visited Stalin at the end of July, Stalin had gotten over his initial fear, and, from all appearances, had decided to fight it out with the hated Germans, come what might from British and American resources. The early speed of the Nazi invasion had already slackened off, the result of increasingly improved resistance from the Russian armies, and there was the certain prospect of the kind of Russian winter that had defeated Napoleon and his troops. Later, Stalingrad would make manifest the kind of war Stalin was willing to wage, at whatever cost in lives, in defense of nation and regime. It is, in sum, exceedingly unlikely that Stalin, as the consequence of a hard policy on the part of Churchill and Roosevelt, would have surrendered to Hitler. Even if his main armies had suffered from lack of materiel from the United States, there were other ways of carrying on the war against Hitler.

It is impossible to understand the wartime White House or even Roosevelt's leadership in the war without reference to Harry Hopkins as friend, adviser, envoy, and trusted confidant to the President, beginning in 1940 when the Roosevelts invited Hopkins and his young daughter to make their home in the White House. Raymond Clapper, newspaper reporter and columnist of the time, who covered the White House and knew both the President and Hopkins, wrote in 1938: "Many New Dealers have bored Roosevelt with their solemn earnestness. Hopkins never does. He knows instinctively when to ask, when to keep still, when to press, when to hold back; when to approach Roosevelt direct, when to go at him roundabout." Robert Sherwood in his *Roosevelt and Hopkins,* from which the Clapper quotation comes, further quoted, from a "distinguished European," the observation that "Hopkins has an almost feminine sensitivity to Roosevelt's moods."[7]

More recently, the admiring biographer of Roosevelt, James McGregor Burns, wrote of Hopkins: "He had almost an extrasensory perception of Roosevelt's moods; he knew how to give advice in the form of flattery and flattery in the form of advice; he sensed when to press his boss and when to listen, when to submit and when to argue."[8]

The shrewd Churchill had realized on his first meeting with Hopkins that to an almost incredible degree, Hopkins could and did speak for the President on almost any subject—something that no Cabinet secretary, especially not Secretary Hull in the State Department, could do. Roosevelt could be ruthless in disavowing overnight something that even the most well-meaning and loyal member of the government had said. He never did that to Hopkins. Hopkins had joined the New Deal as a social work supervisor. He was an ardent liberal-progressive, social democratic if not socialist in his larger mind, and had acquired a certain notoriety as being at one and the same time a zealous New Dealer and also a kind of *bon vivant* with a special fondness for the race track. His attitude toward the Soviet Union was that of the typical liberal-progressive: He regretted that the Soviet Union tended toward totalitarianism, but he was hopeful for its future, given its egalitarian philosophy.

Hopkins travelled widely and often for the President. He was on assignment in London on July 25, 1941, when he asked the President for permission to visit the Soviet Union to have a *tête à tête* with Stalin on Russia's exact war needs. Roosevelt assented immediately. All that Hopkins carried with him, apart from his passport, was a cable he had received just before departure from Under Secretary of State Sumner Welles. It was a cable of official introduction on Hopkins's behalf from Roosevelt to Stalin. The key presidential passage in the cable was: "I ask you to treat Mr. Hopkins with the identical confidence you would feel if you were talking directly to me. He will communicate directly to me the views that you express to him and will tell me what you consider are the most pressing individual problems on which we could be of aid."[9]

Understandably, Stalin rolled out the red carpet for Hopkins, giving him the sort of reception the Soviets reserved for visiting heads of state. There were hours of talk between Hopkins and Stalin attended only by an interpreter. Stalin described the position of the Russian and German armies, indicating that despite all the early Russian reverses, "Germany underestimated the strength of the Russian army." He believed that there would shortly be a significant turn. He did need help, however; a very great deal of help, immediately. He needed a "second front" opened by Britain in France, right away. And he needed huge quantities of military supplies of every kind and description—tanks, planes, guns, special or rare metals for use in Russian factories, ships, food for the Russian people, and so on. Hopkins made detailed lists of Stalin's requests.

Stalin said that he hoped, now that Russia was being invaded by the Germans, that the U.S. would enter the war and fight alongside the Russian troops. America could maintain its own armies independent of the Russians and under strictly American leadership. According to Hopkins, Stalin "repeatedly said that the President and the United States had more influence with the common people of the world today than any other force."

In a mere two days, Hopkins had gained more information from Stalin, had been vouchsafed more of Russian policy and plans, than any foreign visitor in Soviet history. As a *tête à tête* it was matchless, a *tour de force*. After his return to the U.S. to report in detail to the President, Hopkins wrote an article on his meeting with Stalin, in the then popular *American* magazine. It came close to being rapturous:

> Not once did he repeat himself. He talked as he knew his troops were shooting—straight and hard. He welcomed me with a few swift Russian words. He shook my hand briefly, firmly, courteously. He smiled warmly. . . . We talked for almost four hours on the second visit. . . . And when we said good-by we shook hands again with the same finality. He said good-by once, just as only once he said hello. And that was that. Perhaps I merely imagined that his smile was more friendly, a bit warmer. Perhaps it was so because, to his word of farewell, he had added his respects to the President of the United States.
>
> No man could forget the picture of the dictator of Russia as he stood watching me leave—an austere, rugged, determined figure in boots that shone like mirrors, stout baggy trousers, and snug-fitting blouse. He wore no ornament, military or civilian. He's built close to the ground, like a football coach's dream of a tackle. . . . He curries no favor with you. He seems to have no doubts. He assures you that Russia will stand against the onslaughts of the German army. He takes it for granted that you have no doubts either. . . .[10]

Hopkins clearly didn't, ever after. Neither did FDR, once Hopkins had brought back his tidings. A final part of Hopkins's official report was marked "For the President only." In it Hopkins stressed the high respect that Stalin had for him as the preeminent world leader and had also for the United States as the standard-bearer of world progress. Just before his departure from Russia, Hopkins sent a short personal cable to the President in which he reported Stalin's anxiety that an important American loan had not yet been received by the Kremlin and asked that immediate and uninterrupted flow of materiel begin.[11]

It would be hard to exaggerate the importance of the Hopkins-Stalin talks—to Hopkins, the President, and, as things turned out, Stalin himself. Ambassador Steinhardt reported to the State Department that Stalin had talked to Hopkins "with a frankness unparalleled in my knowledge in recent Soviet history on the subject of his mission and the Soviet position."

From the moment it received Hopkins's cabled message, the White House went into almost frenzied activity. On August 1, before Hopkins had even returned, simply on the basis of the brief cable, Roosevelt called a Cabinet meeting in which, according to Harold Ickes's notes, the President "started in by giving the State Department and the War Department one of the most complete dressings-down that I have witnessed." Henry Morgenthau wrote in his diary that the President "went to town in a way I have never heard him go to town before. He was terrific. He said he didn't want to hear what was on order; he said he wanted to hear only what was on the water."[12]

The extraordinary Cabinet meeting was the beginning of a series of declarations and actions on the part of Roosevelt and Hopkins in which the Soviet Union became a favored nation in every possible sense of the phrase. General James H. Burns and Colonel (soon to be Brigadier General) Philip Faymonville were put in special charge of aid to Russia. Faymonville was a favorite of Joseph Davies, though not, apparently, of William C. Bullitt and Loy Henderson, both of whom had "serious doubts" about the Colonel's judgment. But it was Joseph Davies who had the crucial influence in the White House on all Soviet matters, not the likes of Bullitt and Henderson, both vastly more experienced in Soviet matters but rapidly becoming impotent in the White House.[13]

The Soviets repeatedly expressed a preference for "credits" from America instead of inclusion in the lend-lease program. This was because under the latter they were strictly limited, or at least there were strict written limitations—as with Britain—on what they could do in the way of inspecting American factories and of preventing American inspections of their use of American goods. To this end the White House worked valiantly, though ultimately unsuccessfully; Congress preferred the lend-lease route. But the Soviet fetish for secrecy, which would never leave the Kremlin, was at no time more evident than in the fall of 1941 when Roosevelt was giving the Soviets everything he could. Credits—with which letters instead of elaborate forms sufficed to receive money and goods—were much easier to combine with secrecy than lend-lease.

Roosevelt and Hopkins, for their part, wanted as much direct control of Russian aid, and just as little oversight from the established congressional and executive agencies, as was humanly possible. Hopkins, Dawson writes, "was seeking to organize the Soviet aid program in such a manner as to insure its control from the White House, thereby circumventing the countervailing policy approaches entrenched in other Washington quarters."[14]

Roosevelt gave much personal attention to the far from easy task of winning American public opinion over to his Soviet aid cause. In the beginning, after Russia was attacked by Hitler, there were Americans, in civil society and also the military, who found the Soviet Union a more dangerous adversary in the long run than even Hitler's Germany. A general, if often silent, sentiment among Americans was the hope that somehow the two countries fighting in the East would destroy each other, like two wasps in a bottle. Senator Robert Taft spoke to this group in a speech:

> If Hitler wins it is a victory for fascism. If Stalin wins it is a victory for communism. From the point of view of ideology there is no choice.
> But the victory of communism would be far more dangerous to the United States than the victory of fascism. There has never been the slightest danger that the people in this country would ever embrace bund-ism or nazism. . . . But communism masquerades, often successfully, under the guise of democracy, though it is just as alien to our principles as nazism itself. It is a greater danger to the United States because it is a false philosophy which appeals to many. Fascism is a false philosophy which appeals to very few indeed.[15]

It was particularly religious Americans—of whom there were a great many, certainly a substantial majority—that Roosevelt worked strenu-ously to placate and then turn to his own direction in Russian policy. Given the number and influence of the Catholics in America, he went to work on the Vatican. To Myron Taylor, our official representative to the

Vatican, went instructions to notify the Holy See that he, Roosevelt, "is definitely bearing in mind the possibility of persuading the Government of Russia ultimately to accept freedom of religion. . . . At the present time Russia is in no sense the aggressor nation—Germany is."[16] Similar efforts were made by the White House to capture Protestant sympathies, and these bore quicker fruit; a list of a thousand eminent Protestant well-wishers of the Soviets was easily prepared. The liberal Catholic church had not yet come into being in America; but the liberal-progressive Protestant faith was already significant.

Roosevelt's boldest—and, alas, most duplicitous—stroke in behalf of his rising eagerness to convert American opinion was the notorious press conference he called in early November 1941, which included the following exchange:

THE PRESIDENT: As I think I suggested a week or two ago, some of you might find it useful to read Article 124 of the Constitution of Russia.

QUESTION: What does it say, Mr. President?

THE PRESIDENT: Well, I haven't learned it by heart sufficiently to quote—I might be off a little bit, but anyway: Freedom of conscience . . .

QUESTION: Would you say . . .

THE PRESIDENT: Freedom of religion. Freedom equally to use propaganda against religion, which is essentially what is the rule in this country; only we don't put it quite the same way.
   "To illustrate his point, the President continued by pointing out that a sidewalk orator could mount his box on a Washington corner and inveigh for or against religious doctrine. . . ."[17]

This, needless to say, was too much for some of even the most liberal of the interventionists lined up behind Roosevelt on the question of Russia. What the historian Robert Dallek has written is highly apposite:

Roosevelt knew full well there was no freedom of religion in the Soviet Union. Nor was he blind to the fact that he could extend lend-lease help to Russia without demonstrating her devotion to religious freedom. But his concern to associate the Soviets with this democratic principle extended beyond the question of aid to *the problem of American involvement in the war.* Convinced that only a stark contrast between freedom and totalitarianism would provide the emotional wherewithal for Americans to fight, Roosevelt wished to identify the Russians regardless of

Soviet realities, with Anglo-American ideals as fully as he could.[18] (Italics added.)

Such was FDR's desire to win the American people to the Soviet Union, despite its repugnant policy toward religion, that he sought to persuade the Soviet government to make appearances a little more winning, to issue perhaps some kind of war statement affirming that, deep down, appearances notwithstanding, the Kremlin wasn't really opposed to religion. He got nowhere, but such became Roosevelt's desire to connect Stalin with religion that Roosevelt seems to have convinced himself eventually. After his return from Yalta in February 1945, he described Stalin to his Cabinet as having "something else in his being besides this revolutionist, Bolshevik thing." The President went on to tell his rapt audience that this might have something to do with Stalin's early training for the "priesthood." He added: "I think that something entered into his nature of the way in which a Christian gentleman should behave." Roosevelt was of course within weeks of his death; there is no record of the faces of his Cabinet listeners.

Another kind of opposition to limitless generosity to the Soviets came from American military leaders, among them General Marshall. The blunt fact was that America at that time was herself woefully undernourished in almost every department of the military. It was by one vote only that even the limited national conscription that had been agreed to in 1940 was extended—for six months—in the fall of 1941. That is an adequate indicator of the woeful state of military preparedness in America. There was an alarming shortage of almost every conceivable type of military equipment—from rifle ammunition all the way to tanks and planes. Although by this time, late 1941, American factories were working overtime, there were inevitable, unavoidable, shortages for American troops, and these were exacerbated by White House insistence upon huge shipments to Russia. There is a revealing memorandum sent by General Marshall at the end of August 1941 to his chief, Secretary of War Henry Stimson:

In the first place our entire Air Corps is suffering from a severe shortage in spare parts of *all* kinds. We have planes on the ground because we cannot repair them. . . .

"Mr. Oumansky [the Soviet ambassador] and his Russian associates were informed of this situation. . . .

I think the President should have it clearly pointed out to him that Mr. Oumansky will take everything we own if we submit to his criticisms.[19]

We are now in a position to begin to understand the paragraph in Roosevelt's letter to Churchill on March 18, 1942, with which this chapter began, declaring that Stalin liked him better than either the State Department or the British Foreign Office and also that he could "personally handle Stalin." Behind the boastful paragraph lay Hopkins's message that Stalin considered the President the foremost world influence in behalf of the downtrodden and that Stalin would be honored to have the American army fight on the eastern front against the Nazis. That was heady enough news for anyone of large ego. Then there had been Roosevelt's frenetic personal devotion to the cause of lend-lease for the Russians, plus his public efforts to say good things about Stalin's regime.

What other conclusion could Roosevelt draw but that Stalin liked and respected him to a singular degree and that Stalin would deeply appreciate the special intensity with which the White House was working on behalf of Russia. How, Roosevelt must have asked himself as he looked into the mirror, could Stalin fail to like such a President, and how could he fail now at handling Stalin?

As some readers know, and as will become progressively evident in this book, no worse misjudgment of Stalin's nature could have been made by the President. A near career had been made and would continue to be made by the dictator of all Russias based upon exploitation of those who came bearing gifts and seeking friendship. From the mid-1930s such seasoned experts as Loy Henderson, Kennan, and Bullitt, among others, were aware of this pathological but real and unalterable bent of Stalin's. At least two Roosevelt-dispatched ambassadors to the Kremlin, Standley and Harriman, early became aware of Stalin's nature and tried to warn the President, who would not, however, be warned.

Once America was in the European war—courtesy of Hitler's declaration of war on America immediately after Pearl Harbor—Roosevelt lost no time in commencing his courtship of Stalin, through both direct and indirect ploys for the despot's attention. There was much to be done if Roosevelt was to succeed in winning the trust and then the friendship of Stalin. The most important step was that of arranging a meeting somewhere of just the two of them plus an interpreter and the smallest possible staff in attendance. I shall come to Roosevelt's efforts along this line in the next chapter.

Two other means of acquiring Stalin's trust were through the shipment of materiel to Stalin by the dangerous Arctic route to Archangel, and, second, by applying the maximum possible pressure on Churchill to agree to the earliest possible Anglo-American invasion of Nazi-held France. Stalin had pressed upon Hopkins the extreme importance of forcing Hitler to transfer divisions from the Russian front to fight in France. Roosevelt was determined from the beginning to help Stalin in both respects.

He was unrelenting in his insistence that convoys be kept sailing to Russia, despite the terrible toll taken on these fleets in Arctic waters by Nazi ships and planes operating from Norwegian bases. Throughout 1942, the losses of ships, crews, and supplies kept mounting. Stalin refused to offer any assistance from Soviet bases with planes and ships, and was surly to the point of ugliness at any suggestion from Churchill that in the interest of lives and ships there might have to be a reduction in the convoy traffic.

Churchill, often charged with being reckless with the lives of troops, found the toll more and more difficult to endure. There had to be some change, even if it resulted in a reduction in supplies shipped. Roosevelt and Hopkins were, however, adamant that, fearful losses notwithstanding, nothing, repeat nothing must be allowed to cut down on supplies for the Soviets. Supplies must go, whatever the cost, however grim the toll, to Soviet Russia through Arctic waters.

The convoys to northern Russia, with the fearful losses of lives and cargoes, were the subject of the first sharp difference between Roosevelt and Churchill. Martin Gilbert's biography cites "the long and difficult controversy with Roosevelt over the Russian convoys," one, Gilbert writes, that on a couple of occasions sent Churchill to Chartwell for rest and emotional repair.[20]

In the *Correspondence* there are revealing letters between the two men about the limits of accommodating Stalin. On April 24, Churchill wrote Harry Hopkins of his desire to cut down shipments sharply until more protection could be given them. Clearly Churchill hoped to enlist Hopkins's charm in his own effort. But it was Roosevelt himself who replied to Churchill, on April 26.

"I have seen your cable to Harry this morning relative to shipments to Russia, and I am greatly disturbed by this because I fear not only the political repercussions in Russia but even more that our supplies will not reach them promptly . . . any word reaching Stalin at this time that our supplies were stopping for any reason would have a most unfortunate effect."

A deeply concerned Churchill replied May 1: "With very great respect what you suggest is beyond our powers to fulfill. Admiral King has already expressed our opinion that transatlantic escorts are stretched too thin. . . . I beg you not to press us beyond our judgment in this operation which we have studied most intently. . . . I assure you, Mr. President, we are absolutely extended and I could not press the Admiralty further."

Stalin appealed to Churchill to ensure arrival of war goods on ships bottled up in the ice of the Arctic. Churchill replied that everything possible would be done. He added: "I am sure you will not mind my being quite frank" and went on to list some of the kinds of help the Soviet forces could give the convoys in their Nazi-infested waters, including provision of long-range fighters to cover the convoys "for that part of the voyage when they are approaching your coasts, along with anti-submarine patrols by Soviet aircraft and surface vessels."[21] Stalin didn't reply. Nor did he ever take notice of repeated British complaints about the often ugly treatment at Archangel and Murmansk of British sailors who had managed to survive the Arctic route.

Disagreement between Roosevelt and Churchill continued. On July 14, Churchill wrote FDR: "Only four ships have reached Archangel, with four or five more precariously in ice off Nova Sembla, out of thirty-three included in Convoy PQ 17. If half had gotten through we should have persevered, but with only about a quarter arriving, the operation is not good enough. . . . Allied shipping losses in the seven days ending July 13th, including the Russian convoy were reported at not far short of four hundred thousand tons for the week, a rate unexampled in either this war or the last, and if maintained evidently beyond all existing replacement plans."

Roosevelt's sympathy for Stalin was if anything enhanced. He was troubled at the thought of having to tell Stalin that not only must convoys be reduced but also that it looked as though a second front in France couldn't be mounted immediately—a matter I shall return to shortly. When he wrote Churchill on July 29, he said: "We have got always to bear in mind the personality of our ally and the very difficult and dangerous situation that confronts him. No one can be expected to approach the war from a world point of view whose country has been invaded. I think we should try to put ourselves in his place."

At Roosevelt's request Churchill went to Moscow to tell Stalin the bad news, on the convoys and the second front, with Churchill thus put in the position of being the author of this double disappointment for Stalin. Harriman was the main American representative on the trip. As he reported afterward, Churchill began the talk with Stalin by trying to put into perspective the factors compelling a slowing down of the convoy shipments to Archangel and also the postponement of the cross-Channel second front that Stalin wanted to begin immediately, irrespective of the state of British and American means of invasion of the continent. Stalin broke into Churchill's explanation savagely. Referring to the scattering of the rescue of Convoy PQ 17, Stalin told Churchill: "This is the first time in history that the British navy has ever turned tail and fled from the battle. You British are afraid of fighting. You should not think that the Germans are supermen. You will have to fight sooner or later. You cannot win a war without fighting."

Harriman's report of Churchill's reply to Stalin makes for stimulating reading. There were fury, frustration, and indignation among other ingredients. It was, Harriman wrote, "the most brilliant of Churchill's wartime utterances." In his infuriated reply, Churchill took pains to remind Stalin that Britain had fought Hitler alone and had to live with an alliance between the Soviets and the Nazis from 1939 to 1941. Stalin was struck by the Churchill performance to the point where he signaled his interpreter, who couldn't possibly keep up with the speed of Churchill's words in any event, to be silent in order that Stalin could catch the tenor, and the emotion, of Churchill without understanding specific words. Stalin did not again insult Churchill and Britain on the Kremlin visit.[22]

About this time Roosevelt received a request from Ambassador Standley that he be allowed to return briefly to the United States in order to acquaint the President with a "very important matter" on which he preferred to speak personally rather than communicate by cable or letter. Roosevelt immediately agreed, clearly under the supposition that Standley wanted to tell the President in personal detail just how badly off the Russians were and how much they needed American supplies. Roosevelt even wrote Churchill to this effect, indicating that he had instructed Standley to return and that he could easily guess what it was Standley wanted to talk about, to wit, Russia's tragic plight if the convoys were to be reduced in the slightest degree.

Alas for FDR's hopes, Standley came to tell the President that the Soviet leaders were becoming almost impossible in their refusal to cooperate with the Americans and in their overall surliness about America's unconditional aid. The "very important matter" that had led Standley, an old friend of the President, to request permission to come back to Washington was "to try to get the President to modify the American policy of giving unconditional aid to Russia."[23]

Ambassador Standley was not the first nor the last to go to Moscow with high expectations and the belief that courtesy and warmth on his part would melt Soviet sullenness and inspire the Soviets to genuine partnership. Neither was he the first nor the last to discover that Roosevelt was indifferent. Bullitt had; so had Henderson, Kennan, and Bohlen. So would Harriman in 1944. One wonders if Roosevelt held on to his temper when he learned that the "important message" Standley bore was not, as he had implied to Churchill, a threat by the Soviets to withdraw from the war unless they were granted further assistance. The following year Standley was replaced.

Roosevelt was nothing if not persevering. On October 7, he wrote Churchill: "I think there is nothing more important than that Stalin feel that we mean to support him without qualification and at great sacrifice."

An equally important matter on which Roosevelt and the American chiefs sharply disagreed with Churchill and his chiefs had to do with the opening of a second front in the West. From early 1942, the Americans were adamant in their conviction that a cross-Channel invasion of German-occupied France was an immediate necessity. Stalin wanted this, the Communist parties in both England and the United States were resoundingly in favor of it, and so were many ordinary American and English citizens who thought such an operation would be easy and would bring the boys "home by Christmas."

Churchill didn't see the matter in the same light. In the first place, it was not strictly speaking a *second* front. The *true first* front was Britain's own against the Germans, and the actual *second* front was that in the East, in Russia. Thus the proposed cross-Channel invasion would be a *third* front. The British chiefs were united in their belief that 1942 and very probably 1943 were too early for serious consideration of a direct assault on the powerfully held French coast across the Channel. They were well informed about Nazi gun emplacements, air fields, planes, and well trained divisions available to repulse any but the most formidable and meticulously planned attacks. Nor had the British forgotten Dunkirk and the near disaster to Britain in 1940. Beyond these considerations was the fact that Churchill, in company with such renowned British military experts as Major General J. F. C. Fuller especially and also Captain Liddell Hart, had a strong disinclination to repeat the terrible slaughter of direct, head-on field assault that had characterized the First World War.

Neither Roosevelt nor Marshall was particularly mindful of such considerations. American generals from Grant to Pershing had tended to favor the kind of mass assault tactics which were prominent in the Civil War, especially on the Union side in the final two years of the war. Indirection, subtlety, flank attacks, feints, and deceptions, all smacked of evasion of true war and also needless prolonging of a conflict. For both Roosevelt and Marshall, the ideal way of defeating the Germans was an early head-on attack across the Channel. This was the strategy the Army Plans division worked on in the first months of 1942, and by the end of March it was The Plan. On April 1, Roosevelt wrote Churchill: "I have come to certain conclusions which are so vital that I want you to know the whole picture and to ask your approval. The whole of it is so dependent on complete cooperation by the U.K. and the U.S. that Harry and Marshall will leave for London in a few days to present first of all to you the salient points."

Two days later, on April 3, Roosevelt sent another letter to Churchill, adding what he plainly regarded as a kind of bell-in-the-night fillip to the first letter. "What Harry and Geo. Marshall will tell you about has my heart and *mind* in it. Your people and mine demand the establishment of a front to draw off pressure on the Russians, and these people are wise enough to see that the Russians are today killing more Germans and destroying more equipment than you and I put together. Even if full success is not attained, the *big* objective will be."

Big objective? What could that be if not the pleasing of Stalin at whatever cost? Certainly the hazards of a cross-Channel invasion for the then-puny military resources of Britain and the United States were almost infinite. There was no realistic way in which a small military force, equipped with minimal landing and invasion equipment, could crush the well-fortified, well-armed, well-seasoned German soldiers on the other side of the Channel. When we think of all that was required in the way of soldiers, landing craft, mobile harbors, weapons, ammunition, planes, destroyers, and the like in the Allied invasion of France on June 6, 1944, we can only shudder at the thought of anything undertaken in the fall of 1942 and spring of 1943.

Roosevelt recommended that the attack be aimed at "selected beaches" between Le Havre and Boulogne. The main objective would be Antwerp, which was fairly saturated with German divisions and fortifications. Inasmuch as only five American divisions would be "ready" by the fall of 1942, just six months hence, the "chief burden" of the plan must fall on Britain. On 15 September, Roosevelt declared, the United States could provide half the number of troops required but only 700 of the 5700 cover aircraft.

At the conference of Hopkins and Marshall with the British, Marshall pronounced the plan a "definite aim," not simply a proposed operation to be carefully explored with the British—who, after all, knew the Channel better than the Americans—but a considered proposal, firmly arrived at, and now presented to the British virtually as a *fait accompli*. When Brooke pointed out the need for large numbers of landing craft, and their absence—they were then given a low industrial priority by joint American-British agreement—Marshall replied that just before he and Hopkins had departed America, the President, on his own, had instituted a crash program. Marshall was sure that that and other seeming difficulties would work themselves out by early fall. He acknowledged that the number of American divisions would still be rather low by then, but believed it could be compensated for.

Hopkins spoke almost soulfully. The decision to begin the second front across the Channel was one "of the most momentous which had ever been faced." On this decision "depended the preservation of all that democracy held dear." Moreover, declared Hopkins, this decision, once made, could never be reversed. "It would constitute [the Americans's] major effort."[24]

Churchill, all dismay and incredulity concealed, wrote Roosevelt his congratulations on the plan while the London conference was still going on. His letter of April 12 reads in part: "I have read with earnest attention your masterly document about the future of the war and the great operation proposed. I am in entire agreement in principle with all you propose and so are the Chiefs of Staff." This simply was untrue; but not for a second could Churchill risk alienating Roosevelt from his own war policy of Europe First. There was no alternative to a Churchillian strategy of doing everything possible to wean the Americans away from their plan while seeming to praise it.

Brooke asked Marshall what plans there were for the immediate reinforcement of any invasion troops that might scratch their way to a precarious hold on the enemy shore. Marshall said no thought had been given to that; it didn't seem important enough at this juncture. He was sure that once the Americans made their way to the other side, they would find ways to survive.

The historian Mark Stoler, writes of this episode: "The fact that Marshall had not even begun to think about what to do after the landings took place only strengthened Brooke's belief that the plan was merely a political ploy and the American chief of staff a strategic fool. In retrospect, Marshall's memorandum seemed 'fantastic' and, according to one British phrase, 'almost childlike in its simplicity.' "[25]

In any event, it was evident to the British that the vaunted American plan had given no serious thought to the actual strategy, tactics, and logistics of war. It was as though the Americans were still thinking in terms of the early Indian and Mexican wars; not of the kind of warfare waged by Germany since 1939. Marshall and Hopkins were not unaware of the skepticism of Churchill and his associates—skepticism tempered by a strong desire to avoid offending the President.

In the detailed report that Hopkins wrote for the President about the London conference, he emphasized the forcefulness he had used in telling Churchill personally just how eager the President and his chiefs were about the plan. "I made it very plain that our military leaders, after canvassing the whole world situation, made up their minds that this was the one . . . that was by far the most advantageous from a strategic point of view. I impressed as strongly as I could on Churchill that he should not agree to this proposal on any assumption that we do not mean business, nor should he assume that in all probability it will not require the use of ground forces. . . . I particularly stressed . . . that the disposition of the United States was to take great risks to relieve the Russian front."

The Americans, well before Marshall's and Hopkins's visit to London, had foreseen British skepticism and reluctance. Stoler, drawing from the Arnold papers, writes: "As early as April 1, the president and his military advisers had seriously considered the possibility of informing Stalin of the American plan 'without letting Churchill know anything about it.' After 'considerable discussion,' they had decided that 'perhaps it would be better' to talk over the matter with London first."[26]

Both Marshall and Hopkins thought it important to cable Washington from London in order to express their suspicions about Churchill's and his chiefs's reserved acquiescence to the plan. Marshall stressed the lengths to which the Americans would have to go in order to keep the British from waffling on the plan.

We can hardly blame the British. They were only too aware of the grave deficiencies in their American ally's preparation for war of any kind in 1942. The deficiencies began with American leadership. The British chiefs rightly believed that there was not yet genuine strategic field competence on the part of the senior American generals. Later in the war, Churchill minuted his chiefs: "The Arnold-King-Marshall combination is one of the stupidest strategic teams ever seen. They are good fellows and there is no need to tell them this."[27]

Churchill, alas, meant it. He must have reached that conclusion, as did his chiefs, in April 1942 at the conference in London. Marshall, however gifted in both character and administrative leadership, was not in any significant degree a field strategist.

On one occasion when Churchill and his military chief, General Ismay, were on a visit to the U.S. in 1942, they were invited by Secretary Stimson and General Marshall to accompany them on a brief trip to South Carolina to see how well and how quickly trained the American soldiers were. Stimson and Marshall thought they were already at "combat readiness." Churchill and Ismay, however, were far from impressed. Ismay muttered to Churchill that "it would be murder to pit them against continental soldiers." Churchill, after expressing satisfaction at the spirit of the trainees, said: "It takes two years to make a soldier." How right Ismay and Churchill were would be illustrated in Tunisia at the end of 1942.[28]

Molotov came to Washington in late May, after having stopped at London to lay his desires and expectations before Churchill. Churchill had been circumspect and noncommittal in reply to Molotov's demand for a full second front in the West not later than the imminent fall. Roosevelt and his advisers were much more forthcoming. On May 30, Molotov after making it evident that the Soviets expected every square inch of the eastern European territories deeded them by Hitler in the Pact, turned to the prospect of a very early second front. He asked for a "straight answer" on this. FDR turned to Marshall and asked "whether developments were clear enough so that we could say . . . we are preparing a second front." "Yes," replied General Marshall. The President then assured Molotov that he could consider the front now "promised" to Stalin. "Later that day," writes Stoler, "Marshall backed up this pledge by a public statement at West Point that American troops were landing in England and 'will land in France.' "[29]

On June 9, Molotov returned to London on his way back to the

Kremlin. "To the alarm of British policy makers," writes Martin Gilbert, "he had brought with him a Soviet-American draft communiqué with regard to the urgent task of creating a Second Front in Europe in 1942." Morever, the British discovered, Roosevelt had calmly assured Molotov he would be prepared to contemplate a sacrifice of 120,000 men if necessary—British men, as the memoirist Oliver Harvey, present at the scene, added. Churchill dismissed the "communiqué" out of hand.[30]

But Roosevelt had written Churchill on May 31 that the Russian position was precarious and might worsen. "Therefore I am more than ever anxious that Bolero [code name for the proposed cross-Channel assault] proceed to definite action in 1942. We all realize that because of weather conditions the operation cannot be delayed until the end of the year. . . . I believe German airforces cannot be defeated or indeed brought to battle to an extent which will bring them off the Russian front until we have made a landing. I have great confidence in the ability of our joint airforces to gain complete control of the channel and enough of the land for appropriate bridgeheads to be covered. . . . I will telegraph you when Molotov leaves, and I am especially anxious that he carry back some real results of his Mission and that he will give a favorable account to Stalin. I am inclined to think that at present all the Russians are a bit down in the mouth."

In the end, it would be less Churchillian argument than the blunt, inescapable fact that, for all Roosevelt's optimism at the outset, America would not, could not possibly, have enough troops trained and planes, tanks, guns, bombs, and other vital equipment produced to make a cross-Channel operation possible even in early 1943. There was no alternative but to turn to North Africa.

Churchill dispatched in August 1942, almost as if it were an object lesson for American attention, 6,000 well-trained, mostly commando, troops in a surprise night attack on the French port of Dieppe, with depressing results. The Germans repulsed them easily. The British suffered 70 percent casualties, including prisoners-of-war.

For Churchill, North Africa would begin his Mediterranean strategy of moving northward, through Sicily and Italy, in order to penetrate the "soft underbelly" of the German army stretched out from southern Russia to the English Channel. Neither Churchill nor his chiefs saw the Mediterranean move as a substitute for the cross-Channel invasion; it was only seen as a valuable supporting operation. Not before 1944, the British well knew, would preparations for the Channel crossing be completed. In the interim, much could be accomplished through the southern push toward central Europe. For the immediate future, the task was that of defeating the Germans in North Africa—specifically in Tunisia—and using it as a base for the conquest of first Sicily, then Italy.

The results of insufficient American training and experience showed up immediately in Tunisia; almost disastrously at Kasserine. Despite superior numbers and military equipment, the Americans were no match for the Germans. The Americans were routed, with over half of their heavy artillery captured by the German forces. Had it not been for the British troops, the battle for North Africa would have been over before it really began.

Tunisia was eventually secured, and preparations began for the invasion of Sicily. On April 7, 1943, Churchill was astounded to receive from Eisenhower, commanding general of the Sicily operation, a message to the effect that the invasion of the island would have to be postponed until the Allies had greater military strength. Eisenhower had suddenly discovered that there were two German divisions on Sicily. Churchill was furious, knowing full well that there was more than enough Allied power to draw on for the invasion. He telegraphed Hopkins that he found Ike's telegram "most depressing." To his own chiefs of staff Churchill wrote in the form of a minute that Eisenhower's statement "contrasts oddly with the confidence which General Eisenhower showed about invading the Continent across the Channel, where he would have to meet a great many more than two German divisions. . . . If the presence of two German divisions is held to be decisive against any operation of an offensive or amphibious character open to the million men now in French North Africa, it is difficult to see how the war can be carried on. Months of preparation, sea power, and air power in abundance, and yet two German divisions are sufficient to knock it all on the head. I do not think we can rest content with such doctrines."

Churchill still wasn't through. He pointed out that in Eisenhower's first message about the impossibility, even with superior numbers, of attacking the two German divisions and taking Sicily, that both General Montgomery and Field Marshal Alexander agreed with his caution. This turned out to be completely false with respect to Montgomery and largely so with respect to Alexander.

"I trust the Chiefs of Staff will not accept these pusillanimous and defeatist doctrines from whomever they come. I propose to telegraph shortly to the President, because the adoption of such an attitude by our commanders would make us the laughing stock of the world. Especially is this true when, side by side with it, we are urged to attack the French coast across the scour of the Channel."[31]

No telegram of the sort mentioned by Churchill seems to have been sent to Roosevelt. In time, Eisenhower became a more possessed and confident commander in Sicily and Italy, and the American troops became battle-seasoned. Stalin, as may well be imagined, was unhappy at the Allied postponement of the cross-Channel invasion and the wasting—in his eyes—of troops in the Mediterranean.

CHAPTER TWO

"A Meeting of Minds"

Almost from the time Hopkins returned triumphantly from his Kremlin meeting with Stalin in July 1941, Roosevelt seems to have been seized by a desire to have a meeting of his own with Stalin, one that would be secret, limited to the two of them and very small staffs. On April 11, 1942, Roosevelt wrote to Stalin:

> It is unfortunate that geographical distance makes it practically impossible for you and me to meet at this time. Such a meeting of minds in personal conversation would be useful to the conduct of the war against Hitlerism. Perhaps if things go as well as we hope, you and I could spend a few days together next summer near our common border off Alaska. I regard it as of the utmost military importance that we have the nearest possible approach to an exchange of views.
>
> I have in mind a very important military proposal involving the utilization of our armed forces in a manner to relieve your critical Western Front. This objective carries great weight with me. . . .

39

The American people are thrilled by the magnificent fighting of your armed forces and we want to help you more in the destruction of Hitler's armies and materiel than we are doing now.[1]

Receiving no satisfactory reply from Stalin to his first invitation, Roosevelt tried again. He wrote Stalin in early December of the same year. This time he brought Churchill into the proposed discussions, but he still intended a personal and informal meeting of minds. He did not like the idea of a conference of "our military leaders." "I think we should come to some tentative understanding about the procedures which should be adopted in event of a German collapse." It is perhaps relevant here to note that Roosevelt, unlike either Stalin or Churchill, had in his head almost from Pearl Harbor the possibility of a German collapse, though from what cause the Germans would collapse he left airily unexplained. But even though Churchill was included this time in his secret invitation to Stalin, "my most compelling reason," he stated forthrightly, "is that I am very anxious to have a talk with you. My suggestion is that we should meet secretly in Africa. . . ."[2]

Stalin was still uninterested. Roosevelt tried again, telling Stalin "I am deeply disappointed you feel you cannot get away for a conference in January." This time Stalin responded with the suggestion that the three war leaders confer by correspondence. "I do not know as yet what were the specific matters that you, Mr. President, and Mr. Churchill wanted discussed at your joint conference. Could we not discuss them by correspondence until we have an opportunity to meet? I think we shall not differ."[3]

Stalin each time pleaded the press of military matters on his attention, and there is no need to doubt the reality of such pressure, given his largely personal command of the Russian armies. But it is easy to sense that Stalin simply wasn't interested in intimate conversations with Roosevelt. What was in it for him? Tito tells us that Stalin said he didn't trust either Churchill or Roosevelt. Churchill was forever slipping his hand in your pocket to steal a kopeck, but Roosevelt "only goes after the big kopecks." Such a revelation, if it had ever been brought to Roosevelt, just might have crushed him, such was his ardor to accomplish a relationship that could only be effected through a "meeting of minds."

Stalin distrusted Roosevelt and the U.S. from the beginning; there were only two things he wanted: limitless supplies and a very early "second front" across the Channel. How blunt, even curt, Stalin could be, even to

Roosevelt, when extraneous ideas were introduced, is well illustrated by a letter Stalin wrote the President on January 13, 1943. Roosevelt had written Stalin twice to impress upon him the desirability of sending an air unit of a hundred bombers and pilots to be based on Soviet territory in the Far East and also of dispatching General Bradley for the purpose of visiting military bases and munitions factories. Stalin was to the point, to say the least:

> As to sending bomber units to the Far East, I have already pointed out in my previous messages that what we need is not air force units, but planes without pilots, because we have more than enough pilots of our own. Secondly, we need your help in the way of aircraft not in the Far East where the U.S.S.R. is not in a state of war, but on the Soviet-German front. . . .
>
> I was rather surprised at your proposal that General Bradley should inspect Russian military objectives . . . in the U.S.S.R. It should be perfectly obvious that only Russians can inspect Russian military objectives, just as U.S. military objectives can be inspected by none but Americans. There should be no unclarity in this matter.
>
> Concerning General Marshall's visit to the U.S.S.R. I must say I am not quite clear about his mission. Kindly advise me of the purpose of the visit so that I can consider the matter with full understanding and reply accordingly.
>
> My colleagues are upset by the fact that operations in North Africa have come to a standstill and, I gather, for a long time too. Would you care to comment on the matter?[4]

All in all, a letter that must have left the President feeling frustrated in his ardent effort to win Stalin's friendship. Stalin's statement that "U.S. military objectives can be inspected by none but Americans" is comical. There were a considerable number of Russians visiting some of the most secret of American plants and bases, and with the full approval of the White House. But, as will be evident repeatedly, reciprocity was not a familiar notion to Stalin.

On May 5, Roosevelt made yet another, this time very special, effort to win Stalin's assent to a meeting à deux. What was special was not only a letter of unusual personal warmth by himself to Stalin, but the envoy by whom the special letter would be carried: Joseph E. Davies. The U.S. had an ambassador in Moscow, Admiral Standley, but, as we have seen, Standley had irritated Roosevelt by informing him that the Soviets were being increasingly churlish about lend-lease. Even worse, Admiral Standley had later held a news conference in which he spoke critically of Russian behavior. This incensed the President, and that was when he turned to Davies, whom he knew to be *persona grata* at the Kremlin, and who could be depended upon to bear anything from the President to Stalin with great persuasiveness. The President tried his best to persuade Davies to replace Standley as ambassador to the Soviet Union. Davies said his health prevented that, but he would be happy to carry the letter to Stalin.

Davies was given a warm welcome at the Kremlin, the memory of his ambassadorship in the 1930s being still green. He made himself further welcome when, at the state banquet for him, hosted by Stalin, Davies presented his host with a print of the freshly produced movie *Mission to Moscow.* Needless to say, the banquet and the movie afterward were enjoyed by all.

Then, in an atmosphere of almost reverential presentation, Davies, alone with Stalin save for an interpreter, gave him the letter from Roosevelt. Once again, gravely and courteously, Stalin said he was obliged to refuse. The pressure of military affairs on the front necessitated his remaining in Moscow.

Churchill eventually heard about the President's efforts to meet *tête à deux,* and saw the danger immediately. He wrote to Roosevelt on June 25: "You must excuse me expressing myself with all the frankness that our friendship and the gravity of the issue warrant. I do not underrate the use that enemy propaganda would make of a meeting between the heads of Soviet Russia and the United States at this juncture with the British Commonwealth and Empire excluded. It would be serious and vexatious, and many would be bewildered and alarmed thereby. My journey to Moscow with Averell in August 1942 was on altogether a lower level, and at a stage in the war when we had only to explain why no second front. Nevertheless whatever you decide, I shall sustain to the best of my ability."

Roosevelt's reply to Churchill on June 28 opened with a flat lie: "I did not suggest to UJ that we meet alone but he told Davies that he assumed (a) that we would meet alone and (b) that we should not bring staffs to what would be a preliminary meeting. . . . I want to explore his thinking as fully as possible concerning Russia's post-war hopes and ambitions. I would want to cover much the same field with him as did Eden for you a year ago." Eden's visit, unlike Roosevelt's desired one with Stalin, did not, however, take place in secrecy and without intimation to Roosevelt. Nor did it significantly concern the postwar world.

To add sting to Churchill's troubled feelings, he was on the receiving end once again of some of Stalin's harsh accusations of cowardice on the part of Britain. But whatever the fullness of Churchill's feelings about the Roosevelt deception, he could say virtually nothing in protest. America, after all, was in sight of the position she would soon have for the rest of the war: superiority over Britain in the number of troops fighting in Europe, in war production in the U.S., and in economic as well as political power in the world. It had been of utmost importance to Churchill to win the President's support in the early days of the war, and then, chiefly through Roosevelt, the support of the American people. It was entirely due to Roosevelt that most Americans accepted the priority of Germany's defeat over Japan's, despite the fact that the Japanese had attacked the U.S. at Pearl Harbor. Given the whole picture, in short, there was a quickly reached limit to what Churchill could say about almost anything pertaining to prosecution of the war in Europe. The American Joint Chiefs knew this, and were not above dropping hints at their British counterparts about a possible American change of opinion with respect to priority of military theatres.

In January 1943, the President first sprang his idea of announcing the doctrine of unconditional surrender. Elliot Roosevelt was with his father at Casablanca, and has recorded how the inspiration for the doctrine struck him while he was resting in between official sessions. FDR suddenly said "unconditional surrender" out loud, and followed with: "Of course, it's just the thing for the Russians. They couldn't want anything better. 'Unconditional surrender,' he repeated, thoughtfully sucking a tooth, 'Uncle Joe might have made it up himself.' " The President was, Elliot has written, altogether satisfied with the idea and with himself for having thought of it for the war against the Axis powers. He was confident that although Churchill might demur, though not actually oppose the idea, Stalin would be overjoyed at the doctrine.[5]

Roosevelt sprang the idea almost immediately on Churchill who indicated the necessity of his reporting it for approval to his War Cabinet in London, which he did and without any obduracy on the part of the Cabinet. There is reason to believe that Churchill did not much like the doctrine—on the grounds that lead most military strategists and policy-makers to oppose it: It inevitably tends to lengthen a war and is a monumental discouragement to resistance groups working inside the enemy's lines. He was in any event taken by surprise when, on the final day of the Casablanca conference, at the routine press conference, Roosevelt triumphantly announced that unconditional surrender was to be the fate of the Axis powers.

Roosevelt later said that the idea had come to him as he was doing some random musing about the Civil War and General Grant. This reminded him of the fact that after the Civil War, Ulysses S. Grant was often referred to by admirers as "Unconditional Surrender" Grant.[6]

But the President must have been dismayed later in the year when at the first three-power summit meeting at Teheran at the end of November 1943, he was informed by Stalin himself that he didn't like the doctrine, on the ground that it would prevent the Allied nations from using any possibility of negotiating with the German leaders for an earlier surrender. "Speaking about unconditional surrender, Stalin said, as Eden reported to London the following day, that 'he thought this bad tactics vis à vis Germany' and suggested that the Allies work out 'terms' together, and make these known to the German people. Eden added that Churchill 'agrees that this is a better suggestion.' "[7]

Stalin was right; so was Churchill; so have been the majority of military experts in their rejection of the policy of unconditional surrender. But Roosevelt had striven valiantly to please Stalin by promulgating it.[8]

There were, however, many boons and pleasures for FDR at the Teheran summit. In the first place, there would be at last, after a year and a half of trying, the private meetings the President so badly wanted with Stalin, meetings simply to effect, as the President put it, "a meeting of minds." Teheran was the farthest from Moscow Stalin was willing to travel.

The American embassy in Teheran, where the President and his entourage would normally have stayed for the conference, was at least a mile from the Soviet and the British embassies, which were almost side by side. Churchill cabled Roosevelt an invitation, through Stalin, to stay at the British embassy. The President seems not to have received Churchill's cabled invitation. What he did receive was an invitation from Stalin to accept a house within the Soviet embassy compound. Stalin added that his own security officers believed that a German plot was afoot to kidnap the President at the American embassy. The President accepted Stalin's invitation with alacrity.

Only the Soviets appear to have suspected a plot to kidnap the President. The Iranian secret police, the British security force, and the American secret service had no such suspicions. Harriman later wrote that in his opinion there wasn't the slightest threat and the invitation was solely a Soviet ploy to keep the President under complete Russian surveillance. British General Ismay said: "The Soviets had once more got what they wanted," adding "I wonder if microphones had already been installed in anticipation."[9] It is more than likely they had; more than a few Soviet "servants" were observed wearing NKVD uniforms under outer garments of the kind waiters and room maids and others would normally wear.

Nothing could have been better from Roosevelt's viewpoint. He had at last the setting he had so long hoped for: one in which he and Stalin could have a private meeting of minds. As matters worked out, Stalin and Roosevelt had three private meetings just prior to official sessions of the summit meeting. Each man had his interpreter, FDR's being Charles E. "Chip" Bohlen who later wrote up the official minutes of both the private meetings and the official, plenary sessions.

The first of the three meetings began when Stalin and his interpreter came to the President's house within the Soviet embassy compound.[10] The Marshal was impressively courteous, asking the President to feel free to bring up whatever subjects he wished. It was almost foreordained that Poland and its postwar boundaries vis à vis the Soviet Union would be discussed thoroughly by Stalin and Roosevelt in their private meeting. Stalin had early made his views clear to Churchill and Roosevelt. He wanted nothing less than the territories ceded him in his pact with Hitler. Churchill had never said no to Stalin any more than Roosevelt had. We know the Prime Minister was impressed that the Hitler-Stalin Pact put the Russo-Polish line in the vicinity of the Curzon Line that had been recommended by the British at the end of World War I. But we can also reasonably guess that he saw no reason for handing this large part of eastern Poland to the Soviets without some kind of trade. Prior to the Teheran meetings, Roosevelt, for his part, had always taken refuge in his oft-expressed wish that no territorial matters, no spheres of influence, no boundary lines, be discussed at all until after the war in Europe ended.

The subject was very much on the minds of both Stalin and Roosevelt, but it was not until the third of the three private meetings, on December 1, that Roosevelt brought up the matter. He did so, not directly, but as an aspect of his forthcoming run for reelection to a fourth term. He told Stalin that six or seven million Poles lived in the U.S. and as a practical man [he] didn't want to lose their votes. *He said he personally agreed* with the views of Marshal Stalin as to the necessity of the restoration *of a Polish state but would like to see the Eastern border moved further to the West and the Western border moved even to the Oder River.*

He hoped however that the Marshal would understand that for political reasons outlined above, he could not participate in any decision here in Teheran or even, next winter on this subject and that he could not publicly take part in any such arrangement at the present time.

Marshal Stalin replied that now the President explained, he had understood. (Italics added.)

But the President hadn't finished his personal largesse to Stalin. He brought up the Lithuanians, Latvians, and Estonians, all of whom were represented in the United States. He said he fully realized that Russia had had sovereignty over these Baltic States in the farther past and "added jokingly that when the Soviet armies re-occupied these areas, he did not intend to go to war with the Soviet Union on this point." He added that what most concerned Americans was the right of self-determination and that he himself "was confident that the people would vote to join the Soviet Union." Even so, he thought the American minorities concerned would want "some expression of the will of the people, perhaps not immediately after their re-occupation by Soviet forces, but some day." Stalin showed no sign of yielding beyond saying of any plebiscitary indulgence to the peoples involved that "there would be lots of opportunities for that to be done in accordance with the Soviet constitution." Emphatically there would be no international commission brought in. Roosevelt responded that "it would be helpful to him personally if some public declaration in regard to future elections to which the Marshal had referred, could be made."

Behind his stony exterior, Stalin must have been a veritable geyser of geopolitical joys. For here in less than an hour the President had given him what he wanted in Poland and the Baltic States. All Roosevelt had asked in return was that Stalin be sensitive to the needs of Roosevelt's reelection campaign.

It should be stressed here that Roosevelt had what can most charitably be called a blind spot when it came to Europeans, especially eastern Europeans. He had informed Beaverbrook, in Washington, that he favored a plan for rounding up all dispossessed Europeans after the war and resettling them in Africa. He also assured Beaverbrook that people were interested in jobs and security, not territorial boundaries.[11] He also told a Hyde Park visitor one day that he was "sick and tired" of the Poles and other eastern European peoples clamoring about their boundaries and sovereignties. "I'm not sure that a fair plebiscite, if ever there was such a thing, wouldn't show that these eastern provinces would prefer to go back to Russia. Yes, I really think those 1940 frontiers are as just as any."[12]

There was scarcely anything of importance to the official conference, to the Big Three, that wasn't discussed and largely agreed on beforehand by Roosevelt and Stalin in their three private meetings. Truly the "meeting of minds" that FDR wanted was here at last. Roosevelt agreed with Stalin that the large cross-Channel assault by the Anglo-Americans must be set for as early in 1944 as was at all possible and that both an exact date and a commanding officer for that invasion should be set here, now.

Roosevelt introduced at one of the three meetings his cherished idea of a postwar organization of nations, led by what he called the Four Policemen of the world—the U.S., Russia, Britain, and China—that would prevent future national wars. Stalin was skeptical on the grounds that China hardly belonged and that it sounded as though small, relatively unimportant nations would be on equal footing with the superpowers. FDR undertook to dispel Stalin's doubts by assuring him that he agreed with the necessity of curtailing the powers of small nations and that his chief reason for including China among the Four Policemen was its sheer size. It was evident that the President was a good deal more interested in a postwar international organization of any kind than was Stalin. Stalin, however, didn't by any means flout the conception.

France was brought up and instant agreement was reached that France deserved nothing out of the war, given its collaboration under Vichy with the Nazis and its general unreliability in western Europe. Stalin and FDR agreed that France's overseas, imperial possessions, particularly in Indo-China, must be taken from it. Both men made plain that they distrusted de Gaulle.

> Marshal Stalin expatiated at length on the French ruling classes and he said, in his opinion, they should not be entitled to share in any of the benefits of peace in view of their past record of collaborating with Germany.
>
> The President said that Mr. Churchill was of the opinion that France would be very quickly reconstructed as a strong nation, but he did not personally share this view since he felt that many years of honest labor would be necessary before France would be re-established.

The discussion of French imperialism led Roosevelt to mention India to Stalin. "He said that at some future date he would like to talk with Marshal Stalin on the question of India." He thought, however, it was best not to bring up the subject with Churchill. The President said "that he felt the best solution would be reform, from the bottom, somewhat on the Soviet line." (Charles Bohlen, the interpreter, would write years later of this remark that he felt embarrassed for the President in speaking as though the Soviet Revolution had been one "from the bottom up.")

"Marshal Stalin replied that the India question was a complicated one, with different levels of culture and . . . the castes. He added that reform from the bottom would mean revolution."

Today it seems almost hallucinatory, the private meetings between the Chief Executive of the United States and the dictator of the Soviet Union on the spoils of war, not only without Churchill's presence but, so far as FDR could contrive, without Churchill's knowledge of the meetings: *Churchill,* hero of the war against Hitler and staunch adversary of the Nazis even while Hitler and Stalin were embracing, who wanted nothing so much as a close alliance with the United States, a country Churchill loved.

The private talks effectively took the ground out from under Churchill, or for that matter from under the Anglo-American military chiefs so far as their participation in any serious strategy was concerned. The private talks left the official plenary sessions, as Bohlen later wrote, little more than harangues between Stalin and Churchill, with Roosevelt sitting them out and seemingly enjoying them. "I did not like the attitude of the President," wrote Bohlen, "who not only backed Stalin but seemed to enjoy the Stalin-Churchill exchange. Roosevelt should have come to the aid of a close friend and ally, who was really being put upon by Stalin."[13]

Far from feeling any embarrassment over his public partiality to Stalin, Roosevelt seems to have relished it. As he explained to Secretary Frances Perkins when he returned to the White House, the idea of a prank came to him in Teheran, one that would center on Churchill. Roosevelt began one of the official sessions by pretending to whisper to Stalin, loudly enough for the assemblage to hear, that "Winston is cranky this morning; he got up on the wrong side of the bed. A vague smile passed over Stalin's eyes . . . I began to tease Churchill over his Britishness, about John Bull. . . . Winston got red and scowled and the more he did so, the more Stalin smiled. Finally Stalin broke into a deep guffaw, and for the first time in three days I saw the light. I kept it up until Stalin was laughing with me, and it was then I called him 'Uncle Joe.' "[14]

Supposedly Roosevelt had thought to warn Churchill before the meeting began that he was going to act out something that he hoped would cheer Stalin up. But whether he did or didn't alert Churchill in advance, the prank was in the poorest possible taste.

"If the tale is true," writes Keith Eubank, "Roosevelt had insulted Churchill who admired him, and demeaned himself before Stalin who trusted neither man. In his craving for Stalin's approval and friendship, Roosevelt imagined the joke had been on Churchill and that Stalin had laughed with him. More probably Stalin had laughed at the President of the United States belittling an ally to find favor with a tyrant."[15]

From Teheran—more than a year earlier than the more celebrated Yalta—came a cornucopia of delights for Stalin, all with FDR's happy wishes. Roosevelt guaranteed Stalin that he would receive Far Eastern territories in return for Russia's entering the war against Japan after Hitler's defeat. Roosevelt promised Stalin that the Channel invasion of Hitler's France would be supplemented by an invasion of southern France with Anglo-American troops drawn from the Italian campaign, thus wrecking the "soft underbelly" strategy of Churchill and the British chiefs. And finally Roosevelt gave Stalin his assurance that not only Germany but France would be reduced to third rate powers after the war—thus taking away any possible barriers to Stalin's dominant position in western as well as eastern Europe.

Add to the above the priceless realization by Stalin at Teheran—based upon his three secret conversations with FDR and also the unabashed and unvarying support Stalin got from FDR throughout the plenary sessions—that beneath the surface of Anglo-American unity and amity lay very real fissures, profound differences of opinion between Churchill and Roosevelt and the British and the American military chiefs. In this last, vital respect, Teheran can be compared with Munich in 1938. That was when Hitler realized how paper thin the alliance was between Britain and France and, with that realization, made plans immediately for war the following year. At Teheran, Stalin really began the Cold War, and did so on the basis of perceptions identical with those of Hitler at Munich. What would take place at the later Yalta summit meeting would be little more than a formalizing, a moralizing, to cover what had essentially been decided between Roosevelt and Stalin at Teheran.

All in all, Teheran was a virtuoso performance by Stalin. On the way to Teheran, Hopkins had told Alexander Cadogan, of the British delegation, that "you will find us lining up with the Russians."[16] To help launch that lining-up, Roosevelt had refused Churchill's expressed wish for a conference between the two of them on the way to Teheran, just as he refused Churchill's request for just one such meeting, over lunch, at Teheran. General Brooke, Churchill's chief of staff said to Cadogan at the beginning of the Teheran summit: "This conference is over when it has just begun. Stalin has the President in his pocket."[17] And Admiral King of the American chiefs said at the end: "Stalin knew just what he wanted when he came to Teheran and he got it."[18]

Chip Bohlen, Roosevelt's interpreter throughout the Teheran meetings, both secret and open, wrote after the war: "I don't think Roosevelt had any real comprehension of the great gulf that separated the thinking of a Bolshevik from a non-Bolshevik, and particularly from an American. He felt that Stalin viewed the world somewhat in the same light he did."[19]

Churchill saw it all, or most of it, coming. On his way to Teheran he told Harold Macmillan: "Germany is finished, though it may take some time to clean up the mess. The real problem is Russia. I *can't* get the Americans to see it." Sir John Wheeler-Bennett, after thus citing Churchill to Macmillan, adds: "Throughout the Teheran conference Mr. Churchill's depression increased. He was depressed by the all too apparent rapacity of the Soviet claims, at the degree of acquiescence with which these were received by the President and by his own dilemma. For although he alone knew the magnitude of the danger involved, he knew too that he was powerless to avert it. Committed by inclination and policy to maintaining a solidly unified Anglo-American front, he was faced with a situation in which American policy chimed in more often with that of Stalin than with his own. He was thus compelled, usually against his better judgment, to concur in decisions which he felt inimical to the interests of Europe in general and Britain in particular."[20]

There was little if any effort by either Stalin or Roosevelt to disguise the turn things were taking at the expense of Churchill and the British. At the banquet of November 29, the Bohlen minutes report a particularly sharp attack on Churchill. "The most notable feature of the dinner was the attitude of Marshal Stalin toward the Prime Minister. Almost every remark he addressed to the Prime Minister contained some sharp edges. . . . He apparently desired to put and keep the Prime Minister on the defensive. At one occasion he told the Prime Minister that just because Russians are simple people it was a mistake to believe that they were blind and could not see what was before their eyes."[21]

Matters for Churchill were not improved by some serio-comic dialogue between Stalin and the President. Stalin said that at the end of the war, 50,000 German officers should be selected for execution. Churchill was shocked and horrified at the idea. Roosevelt, elaborately playing the role of arbitrator, said that Stalin's figure was too high; that it should be 49,000 officers executed. Churchill left the room in disgust, although Stalin and Molotov saw fit to reassure him that it was all a joke. On returning to the dining room, Elliot Roosevelt declared loudly that he favored executing at least 100,000 German officers. At this Stalin went over to put his arm approvingly around Elliot's shoulders.[22]

It all left a state of depression in Churchill. Throughout the banquet Stalin had railed against France as well as Germany, declaring that the former deserved dismemberment and other devastations with Germany when the war was over. He was emphatic that he thought both the President and the Prime Minister were too kindly disposed to both countries. It was apparent to Churchill that every effort would be made by Stalin to extend Soviet control into western Europe and to crush all possible resistance to it. Without even France left intact after the war, there was not the slightest possibility of keeping the Soviet military forces from invading the West, thus once again confronting Britain, as Germany had in 1940, with the certainty of standing alone against what he had referred to as the "measureless barbarism" of the Soviet Union in a memorandum to Eden.

Lord Moran, Churchill's wartime personal physician, has left in his diary an account of Churchill's deep depression after the banquet. In his rooms, Churchill told Moran there "might be a more bloody war. I shall not be there. I want to sleep for billions of years." Moran continues: "He could not rid himself of that glimpse of impending catastrophe. Blurred and ill-defined as it was, it stuck in his mind. He pulled up abruptly, so that he stood looking down at me, his eyes popping. 'I believe man might destroy man and wipe out civilization. Europe would be desolate and I may be held responsible.' "[23]

There is a more cheerful reaction by Churchill to the Teheran reality he was confronted with. In a letter to an old friend he said that he was the British donkey seated in between the Russian bear and the American buffalo, he alone knowing the way but powerless to act.

* * *

One of President Roosevelt's richer gifts, or attempts at gifts, to Stalin was one third of the captured Italian Fleet—something he offered entirely on his own initiative, without consulting or notifying Churchill. After the surrender of Italy, the acting Italian government approved the request of the Fleet Commander to become a kind of co-belligerent in the Mediterranean war against the Nazis. The Italian Fleet, had been given the status of ally—captive ally, if we choose—in Britain's and America's share of the war against the Germans.

At the Foreign Ministers Conference in Moscow in October 1943, Molotov requested a few of the Italian ships for primary use in northern waters; specifically, he asked for one battleship, one cruiser, eight destroyers, and four submarines to be dispatched at the earliest possible time to the Soviet northern ports; he also asked for 40,000 displacement tons of merchant ships. That was the entirety of the Soviet request, and it came to far, far less than one third of the Italian Fleet.[24] The first, and eminently proper, response of Secretary Hull was to say that he would refer Molotov's request to the next summit meeting of the three heads of government. (This was less than a month distant, at the Teheran summit.) Molotov was dissatisfied, however, at thought of any delay, and protested. His unhappiness was duly reported to the White House.

The very first reference to "one third of the Italian Fleet" seems to be Harry Hopkins's. He drafted the President's response to Hull and in so doing wrote: "One third of the naval ships and one third of merchant ships captured from Italy will be turned over to Russia for their use at the earliest possible moment." This was on October 30, and on that same day two communications went forth from Roosevelt to Hull. In one there was no reference to the "one third," only to satisfying Molotov's request now, without waiting. But the second Presidential communication to Hull, of the same date, included the statement "I hope the Soviets can use their third, and I see no reason why they should not do so."[25]

There the matter rested, without action, until it was discussed once again, this time at the Teheran conference, with Stalin, Churchill, and Roosevelt participating in the discussion. Stalin reaffirmed Molotov's request, and Churchill, without saying no or maybe, said that in order to prevent a possible mutiny and even a scuttling of ships by the Italian Fleet Command—because the Italians might object to this transfer of ships—it would be necessary to speak first to the Fleet Command and to proceed "like a cat handling a mouse." This, let the reader bear in mind, had nothing whatever to do with a *third* of the fleet, only with the number and kind of ships Molotov had requested a month earlier. All Stalin asked was that the ships be on the way to the Soviets by the end of January, no later.

About three weeks after the Teheran meeting, on December 21, Roosevelt wrote Churchill to say that Harriman at Moscow was pressing him for clear and positive word on the ships the Soviets had asked for. Roosevelt told Churchill that he had replied as follows to Harriman:

> It is my intention that Italian surrendered ships to a number of one third of the total be allocated commencing about one February to the Soviet war effort as rapidly as they can be made available from their present employment in the Allied War Effort. After the surrender of our common enemies the title of ownership will be decided.
>
> I have requested Combined Chiefs of Staff to issue necessary orders.

This must have lifted Churchill out of his chair. At no time had there been a discussion of "one third" of the Italian fleet, not with Churchill himself, not with the Combined Chiefs. Yet here was Roosevelt, on his own, in effect telling Harriman to notify Molotov that one third of the Italian fleet would be forthcoming. There was apprehension and bewilderment everywhere. As Roosevelt conceded in a letter on January 8, the Combined Chiefs were dead against the gift on the ground that all Italian ships might well be needed in forthcoming Allied actions. Moreover Harriman had assured him that he understood the "one third" reference to be simply to FDR's own personal intent, not really an order.

Churchill, in his letter to the President of January 16, 1944, wrote that "My recollection is clear that nothing was said at Teheran about 'one-third' but that promise was made to meet the Russian claim put forward at Moscow to have transferred to them one battleship, one cruiser, eight destroyers, four submarines, and forty thousand tons of merchant shipping." Churchill added that he agreed with the Combined Chiefs's dislike of giving any ships at the present time, until it was clear what would be required in operations already planned. "I think very likely that once Stalin is convinced of our intentions and our good faith he will leave us to handle the matter in smoothest and swiftest way possible."

There the matter stood until like a bombshell there fell on Churchill's desk on March 3 a report from Reuters that the President had called a press conference the day before in which he had "given" one third of the Italian fleet to Stalin. "President Roosevelt today announced," read the press report, "that Italian warships are ready to be sent to the Russian navy. Discussions for transferring roughly $1/3$ of the Italian Fleet to Russia, the President said, were about half completed. . . . President Roosevelt explained that since Italy surrendered to the U.S., Britain, and Russia, it was thought advisable to distribute the Italian Fleet roughly on the basis of $1/3$ each."[26]

Churchill's answering message, as he dictated it—though he decided against actually sending it to Roosevelt—was angry and curt: "Can this be true? If so it surprises me very much as it is a complete departure from all our arrangements and agreements. I should be most grateful if you would let me know what has happened, as I shall have to make a statement of my own both to the public and to the Russians. Considering Great Britain has suffered at least twenty times the naval losses of your Fleet in the Mediterranean and has been fighting the Italians since June 1940, we had hoped to be consulted or at least informed beforehand."[27]

Both the French and Greek governments protested Roosevelt's press announcement on the ground that their own losses in the Mediterranean had been substantial. The Italian government also disapproved of Roosevelt's announcement. On March 7, Churchill dictated, and did dispatch, what is probably the nearest to an angry letter he ever wrote the President. It begins: "I have never agreed nor have you ever asked me to agree to a division of the Italian Fleet into 3 shares. . . . His Majesty's government would not be able to agree to a division of the Italian Fleet by $1/3$ or a pro rata division among signatories. . . . We bore the whole weight of that war from 1940 onwards until British and American troops entered Tunisia. . . . Our naval losses have been very heavy indeed." Which they were: among the British naval losses in the Mediterranean between the beginning of the war and the surrender of Italy were a battleship, two aircraft carriers, 14 cruisers, 48 destroyers, and 40 submarines. Churchill's March 7 letter continues:

> We have borne the whole burden of warship losses in the Russian convoys. . . . Up to the present I have been content to leave these matters for adjustment at the end of the war. . . . I therefore suggest that all further discussion of a division of the Italian Fleet, apart from what we agreed with Stalin at Teheran, stand over till the end of the war, when no doubt the Japanese Fleet will also come into consideration.

Churchill reminded Roosevelt that the Russians had asked for one battleship, one cruiser, eight destroyers, and four submarines plus 40,000 tons of merchant shipping. "At Teheran we assented to this. . . . I am sure you will recognize that the British Admiralty made a generous contribution to the plan by providing in fact 13 warships out of the 14 and half the merchant tonnage."

It was clearly important that somehow Roosevelt's dignity be preserved, and Churchill tried valiantly, pointing out that despite the press conference announcement, "Averell [Harriman] was able to assure you that nothing of the sort had been said to the Russians. See your [letter] number 437. You are therefore quite uncommitted so far as they are concerned." Indicating that he would probably have to make a statement to Parliament about the whole matter, Churchill included a draft of what his remarks would be, subject of course to the President's approval. The draft begins: "As President Roosevelt has said, the question of the future employment and disposal of the Italian Fleet has been the subject of some discussion. . . . On these discussions I have no statement to make other than to say that at present no change is contemplated in the arrangements with the Italian Naval Authorities under which Italian ships and their crews take part in the common struggle against the enemy in the theatres where they now operate. . . ."

Thus, helped by Churchill, Roosevelt was able to beat a dignified retreat from his announcement to the world that he would give the Soviets one third of the Italian navy, an announcement that his own military chiefs along with Harriman and other advisers had found unacceptable. Not for the first or last time, the President might have found consolation in the thought that at least Stalin would know how hard he had tried. In any event, a potentially serious crisis had been resolved by Churchill's insight and tact. In the end, it was Britain that contributed all but one of the ships that had been promised Stalin at Teheran.

Still another episode with at least a few roots deep in the Teheran conference was the unleashing by Secretary of the Treasury Henry Morgenthau of his plan for the complete pastoralization of Germany. Morgenthau advocated that the victorious Allies strip all industrial equipment from Germany and permanently occupy the country. Morgenthau triumphantly introduced this plan before Roosevelt and Churchill and their staffs at the Second Quebec Conference, 11–16 September 1944.

At Teheran, Roosevelt had agreed with Stalin that Germany must be dismembered and perhaps divided into a half dozen or more small and separate states. It had also been agreed between the two leaders that

Germany must not have any technology capable of manufacturing weapons and other war materiel. Even a watch-making industry could, Stalin noted solemnly, be easily converted into a weapons producing establishment. Roosevelt agreed with Stalin that Germany must be thoroughly emasculated and—along with France—made incapable of ever again exerting any kind of significant power, military or industrial, in Europe. Roosevelt's ready assent to Stalin's views on both Germany and France, and on the necessity of crippling them permanently, was given warmly during the private sessions with Stalin, and was then reaffirmed when the subject was brought up by Stalin during the official meetings. Churchill tried hard to exclude France from such crippling, but it was a futile effort at the time. Roosevelt's policy hinged upon his constant desire to please Stalin and a general personal dislike of the French, especially General de Gaulle (who was unimpressed with Roosevelt and his generals and doubtless showed it).

In any event, Secretary Morgenthau, during the year following Teheran and preceding the Second Quebec Conference, could work assiduously preparing his plan for the pastoralization of Germany in the knowledge that the President did not think ill of its outline. It was described by one American supporter as a plan for "a pastoral people with factory workers replaced by shepherds and goat herders." Churchill immediately declared his opposition. "I'm all for disarming Germany, but we ought not prevent her living decently. There are bonds between the working classes of all countries, and the English people will not stand for the policy you are advocating. I agree with Burke: You cannot indict a whole nation."[28]

But in the end, even Churchill signed approval, along with Roosevelt. He couldn't avoid it. A badly needed credit of more than six billion dollars from the U.S. was cunningly linked to the Morgenthau plan. Churchill doubtless told himself as he signed the infamous proposal that it couldn't conceivably be accepted by the Americans in the end. And Churchill proved correct. Both Secretary Stimson and Under Secretary McCloy were disgusted with Morgenthau's plan and also his unilateral presentation of it at Quebec, and began lining up strong opposition to the plan immediately—gaining helpful assistance from Felix Frankfurter. The essence of the Morgenthau plan was quickly leaked to the press, with an uproar of protest from most of the press and public following. McCloy drafted a strong memorandum for Stimson arguing the inconsistency of the plan with the Atlantic Charter declaration that "victors and vanquished alike are entitled to freedom from economic want." By the end of

September, the President was vacillating, declaring that "no one wants to make Germany an agricultural nation," and a couple of weeks later he buried the plan in indefinite postponement.

Two years later, McCloy, visiting Churchill at his country home, brought up the Morgenthau plan. Churchill "hastily repudiated it," McCloy wrote in his journal. "Damned Morgenthau and the Prof [Lindeman]—said they were Shylocks."[29] Even in the end of this preposterous affair, we can suppose that Roosevelt reflected yet again that Stalin would know that he had tried.

No episode in World War II is uglier in the light cast on Stalin's viciousness and Roosevelt's deference, if not actual cravenness, to Stalin than the Warsaw Uprising that began in early August 1944 and continued for about three months. From the time the Nazis occupied Poland they faced a courageous resistance movement. By 1944, the Polish resistance became known as the Home Army; among other contributions to the war, the Home Army gave important aid to the Soviet forces around Lublin.

Stalin hated the Polish Home Army because it was loyal to the Polish government-in-exile based in London. It was this government that properly called for an International Red Cross commission to investigate the mass grave of several thousand Polish officers—the discovery of which was announced by the Germans in 1943—who had been barbarically executed by the Soviets back in the winter of 1939. In all, some 15,000 Polish officers were killed, about a third in the Katyn Forest, the others in Siberia where they had been shipped in box cars.

Stalin responded to the Polish government call for a Red Cross commission by furiously breaking off relations with the official Polish government and creating a puppet government based in Lublin. It was the only "government" recognized by the Soviets, and such was their influence that in the end it was the government recognized at Yalta by America and Britain.

In late July 1944, as the Soviet army advanced toward Warsaw, Radio Moscow secretly urged the Warsaw Home Army to revolt against the Germans, promising to make immediate union with the Polish army as the very large Red Army drew near.[30] The Home Army commenced its armed revolt exactly as advised by Radio Moscow, but as the Red Army approached Warsaw it began to slow down, coming to a complete stop at the Vistula river. After a brave and altogether remarkable beginning in which the Home Army actually took command of most of the city, the

Germans threw in heavy reinforcements, especially from the air, and over a three month period gradually wore down and destroyed the Home Army. In the meantime, the Soviets sat and sat, presumably enjoying the spectacle of the hated Polish Home Army being defeated and cruelly destroyed.

This was when an opportunity opened to the British and Americans to give aid to the Polish Home Army in the form of munitions, food, and medicine dropped by Anglo-American planes. These planes needed to use the American air fields in Russia, near the Polish border, in order to refuel before returning to Britain and obtaining fresh supplies. To be able to make use of these air strips loaned by the Soviets, it was necessary to obtain Stalin's approval, but he refused to give it, and he made it evident that he did not approve of the efforts proposed by Churchill to give aid to the Polish forces in Warsaw.

Averell Harriman, U.S. ambassador to the Soviet Union, immediately supported Churchill's call to aid the Poles and implored Molotov to allow the British and American planes to operate. He even promised to make a public declaration that the Soviets, though allowing the relief action, did not sanction it. Harriman's efforts were, however, to no avail. Stalin insisted that the Polish uprising against the Germans was very anti-Soviet and that there was secret collusion between the Poles and the Nazi troops—something grimly denied by the dreadful toll of Polish lives, civilian as well as military, that mounted through August and September.

Churchill and Roosevelt corresponded frequently about assisting the Poles. Always, however, the correspondence shows Churchill proposing, suggesting, and desiring such aid, and Roosevelt protesting, depreciating, or simply refusing to go along. Here, as in other episodes during the war, the President revealed his callousness toward eastern Europeans; a callousness punctuated by interest whenever the election returns in the Midwest dictated.

On August 25, 1944, Churchill wrote Roosevelt an unusually eloquent plea for their joint assistance of the Poles. Churchill enclosed a draft letter to Stalin for both of them to sign which read in part:

> We are most anxious to send American planes from England. Why should they not land on the refueling ground which has been assigned to us behind the Russian lines without inquiry as to what they have done in the war? This should preserve the principle of your government's dissociation from this particular episode. . . . We do not try to form an opinion about the

persons who instigated this rising which was certainly called for repeatedly by radio Moscow. Our sympathies are, however, for the 'almost unarmed people' whose special faith has led them to attack German guns, tanks, and aircraft. We cannot think that Hitler's cruelties will end. . . . On the contrary, it seems probable that that is the time when they will begin with full ferocity. The massacre in Warsaw will undoubtedly be a great annoyance to us when we all meet at the end of the war. Unless you directly forbid it, therefore, we propose to send the planes.

It was a masterly draft: compassionate to the Poles, tactful to Stalin, but firm and helpful, and decidedly action-oriented, as the final sentence indicates. It was, above all, mild in tone. But Roosevelt's reply was immediate and negative.

In consideration of Stalin's present attitude in regard to relief of the Polish Underground in Warsaw as expressed in his messages to you and me, and his definite refusal to permit the use by us of Soviet air fields for that purpose, and in view of current American conversations in regard to subsequent use of other Soviet bases, I do not consider it advantageous in the long range general war prospect for me to join with you in the proposed message to U.J.

On September 4, Churchill, representing the British War Cabinet, wrote again to Stalin requesting compassion for the innocent Polish civilians being slaughtered by the Germans in Warsaw: "Whatever the rights and wrongs about the beginnings of the Warsaw rising, the people of Warsaw themselves cannot be held responsible for the decision taken. Our people cannot understand why no material help has been sent from outside to the Poles in Warsaw. . . . Your government's action in preventing this help being sent seems to us at variance with the spirit of Allied cooperation to which you and we attach so much importance both for the present and the future." Churchill sent a copy to FDR.

Roosevelt wrote Churchill one day later indicating that his intelligence had informed him that the fighting Poles were now out of Warsaw and no help was needed now. He concluded piously: "I have long been deeply distressed by our inability to give adequate assistance to the heroic defenders of Warsaw and I hope that we may together still be able to help Poland be among the victors in this war with the Nazis."

Poland, FDR might have remembered, was the greatest single territorial and substantive symbol of the whole war. After all, it was Hitler's sudden invasion of Poland that had led England and France to declare war on Germany in September 1939. The cruelty that was visited upon the Poles by the Nazis to the end of their occupation, was the greatest moral issue of the war prior to the discovery by Allied soldiers of the death camps for Jews and other Europeans in the early spring of 1945.

On Roosevelt's general attitude toward Poland, the following words by George Kennan are apposite:

> But one does not get—at least I do not—the impression that Roosevelt had any substantive objections—any real political objections—to seeing these areas go to Russia, or indeed that he cared much about the issue for its own sake. One gets the impression that it seemed to him of little importance whether these areas were Polish or Russian. His anxiety was rather that he had a large body of voting constituents in this country of Polish or Baltic origin.[31]

The largest bone of contention by far between Churchill and Roosevelt was the so-called Mediterranean strategy. As Churchill conceived the strategy it was aimed foremost at the Germans, but it contained also the shrewd desire by Churchill to see Allied armies reach central Europe before the advancing Russian armies from the east did. It was important, Churchill said, for the Anglo-American armies and the Soviet armies "to shake hands as far east of Germany as possible."

This aspect of the Mediterranean strategy was identical with what Churchill called the "soft underbelly" approach. At his first conference in Moscow with Stalin, Churchill sought to persuade Stalin of the merits of a campaign northward from the Mediterranean, through Italy primarily. At a certain point in his argument Churchill, with map and pencil, drew an alligator over the German armies as these were stretched out from the Russian border to the Channel coast in the West. He had the snout of the alligator in the West, its long tail in the East. Observe, said Churchill, the soft underbelly of the beast, waiting, so to speak, for attack from the Anglo-American armies now in the Mediterranean area. Churchill made it plain—as he was obliged to repeatedly in the two years prior to the invasion of Normandy in June 1944—that he offered this plan *not in place of* the cross-Channel attack but as yet another front on which the Anglo-Americans could fight the German armies and help take their heavy weight off the Russians. Stalin, we learn, seemed to be impressed, to compliment Churchill on the idea, but it was not long before he changed his mind inflexibly.

The reason is hardly difficult to find. Granted that the effect of the Allied push to the north, whether from Italy, or Greece, or Jugoslavia, would be surely felt by the Germans; so would it eventually by the Russians who would soon be pushing the Germans back as fast as possible in order to take, and keep under Soviet suzerainty, eastern and much of central Europe. Stalin must have realized this a moment after he had praised Churchill's plan at their Kremlin meeting. He never praised it again. In fact it was from approximately that point on that Stalin began to work assiduously toward an abandonment by the Anglo-American forces of their Mediterranean strategy, specifically the strategy of going up Italy to the Po and then beyond to central Europe. The reason why Stalin worked unremittingly on this discouragement and prevention of the northward, "soft underbelly" strategy is contained in a memo that Churchill sent to his chiefs of staff on 9 September 1944, well after the Normandy invasion. "Once again I draw attention to the extreme importance on grounds of high policy of our having a stake in central and southern Europe and not allowing everything to pass into Soviet hands with the incalculable consequences that may result therefrom."[32]

That was the essential basis of the strategy Churchill spent the war trying to persuade Roosevelt to help him implement. It is safe to say that had Churchill's vision been allowed to prevail, the postwar history of eastern Europe and also central Europe, not to forget the Cold War against the West, would be somewhat different.

Stalin began a two-pronged assault on the Churchill strategy: first, to prod incessantly Churchill and Roosevelt (who needed no prodding, of course) for the earliest conceivable date for the great assault from the West, the so-called second front; second, to divert the Anglo-American troops now making their way up Italy to southern France. The southern France operation would be pushed by Stalin as being indispensable to the main invasion in northern France, OVERLORD, across the Channel.

Before turning to Stalin's unfolding of these two steps at Teheran, something additional should be said about Churchill's reasoning in his "soft underbelly" strategy, which came from his experience in World War I.

Almost from the beginning of that war, Churchill was appalled by the dreadful slaughter that went with a trench war in which the Allies and the Germans were in head to head, frontal assault. That led to Churchill's famous, or notorious, Dardanelles strategy of landing Allied troops where they could strike the German forces on Germany's southern flank.

This, Churchill believed, would cut down on the ghastly slaughter and speed up the war. It probably would have, but, sad to say, the execution of his strategy by a stubbornly stupid military command ended in disaster—the Dardanelles disaster that spelled the end of Churchill's high place in the war-government. He promptly and valiantly put on his uniform and went to the trenches in France, to "bloody, muddy France" and its unending harvest of death by the ton—daily, weekly, monthly.

Churchill never forgot that hideous slaughter and its toll of an entire generation of British youth. Without much doubt, Churchill resisted, at least in his deepest mind, the idea of OVERLORD and its possible subjection of another generation to the mass slaughter his generation had known in World War I. From Martin Gilbert comes an interesting and touching story about an evening, well before D-Day and Normandy had taken place, when he escorted the American Under Secretary John McCloy through the badly war-damaged House of Commons. According to McCloy, Churchill ruminated aloud on the devastation of war in general but particularly in World War I when, as he put it, "an entire generation of British manhood" had been wiped out, including some of the cream of British genius and leadership. Churchill went on to say that he, as a survivor from his generation, did not take lightly the prospect of seeing it happen once more—this time perhaps ruinously for Britain's future. "He then said," added McCloy, "that if I felt, or if my Chief, Mr. Stimson felt, that he was using all his efforts to avoid another such slaughter as had taken place in World War I, due to inadequately equipped men, it was not a false accusation. . . . Churchill had spoken . . . [with] great conviction and vigor."[33]

But Roosevelt and Marshall saw the Mediterranean strategy as little more than an evasion of the "real" war, which was crossing the Channel in the face of heavily armed fortifications and an impressive number of mobile, seasoned German divisions, and having it out with them. Moreover, FDR, Marshall, and other American strategists couldn't rid their minds of the deep conviction that Churchill's vaunted strategy amounted to an elaborate means of saving the British Empire, using the Americans as catspaws. What Roosevelt wanted from Churchill was his agreement to General Marshall being appointed supreme commander of not only the forthcoming Normandy invasion but the whole Mediterranean operation as well, thus making it easy to scuttle the Mediterranean strategy. On November 9, 1943, Roosevelt proposed such a single command, and Churchill astutely turned him down immediately.[34]

But all this digested, the fact remains that Churchill did begin to make some headway in his efforts to educate the Americans in grand strategy in Europe. On the eve of the Teheran summit meeting at the end of November 1943, Roosevelt and Eisenhower, if still not the stubborn and suspicious Marshall, began to see the light. The American successes in Italy—after the ragged start in Tunisia—made a difference. At Cairo on November 26, three days before the Teheran summit, Eisenhower, who had been one of the most voluble critics of the North African and Mediterranean policy, declared that "Italy was the correct place in which to deploy our main forces and the objective should be the Valley of the Po. In no other area could we so well threaten the whole German structure, including France, the Balkans, and the Reich itself. Here also our airforce would be closer to the vital objectives in Germany."

As if that were not enough support for the Mediterranean strategy, Eisenhower, who was addressing the Joint Chiefs, went on to say that after the Italian offensive, "the next best method of harrying the enemy was to undertake operations in the Aegean."[35]

Churchill, needless to say, was enormously encouraged by what seemed to be the new view of the Mediterranean as a vital theatre of war, one to be seen not as a substitute for a cross-Channel operation but as a worthy and equally important deployment of Allied forces. He had been deeply concerned that the Americans would want to begin robbing troops and materiel from Italy in order to build up resources for the Normandy invasion. On his way to Cairo, Churchill had been eloquent on the possible "enfeebling effect" on the Anglo-American troops fighting their way up Italy if the rumor began to spread that they were nothing but a glorified feint, with the real action happening across the Channel in the spring. Churchill therefore proposed "for action, that all further movement of British troops and British and United States landing craft from the Mediterranean should be stopped. . . ."[36]

Roosevelt seems to have been persuaded while in Cairo by Churchill's logic. Churchill sent King George an optimistic report on his and the President's agreement. Roosevelt even vouchsafed his confidence that Stalin might well "suggest that we stage an operation at the top of the Adriatic with a view to assisting Tito." That night Churchill cabled the King: "I am making good progress with the President and his high officers, and I am pretty sure all will end up harmoniously."

But all that changed enormously after the President reached Teheran, stayed at the Soviet embassy, had his first private meeting with Stalin, and sat at the first plenary session of the Big Three and their staffs. Stalin didn't waste a moment. He declared that first priority in the West should be the setting of a firm, fixed date for OVERLORD, with full planning and preparation to begin at once—including immediate appointment of the general who would be in supreme command. Stalin said he thought it better to take "OVERLORD as the basis for all 1944 operations; that after the capture of Rome the troops relieved might be sent to Southern France and . . . might eventually meet in France the main force of OVERLORD from the north."[37]

Churchill immediately protested Stalin's recommended abandonment of the Italian campaign by diverting troops to southern France. But Roosevelt was quick to join in with Stalin. He said "that he thought the question of relative timing was very important and that he personally felt that nothing should be done to delay the carrying out of OVERLORD which might be necessary if there were any operations in the Eastern Mediterranean . . . undertaken. He proposed . . . that the staffs work out tomorrow morning a plan of operations for striking at Southern France."[38]

So much for the bloom of Cairo. Stalin had spoken, giving us the bizarre spectacle of Stalin laying down western European as well as eastern European military strategy. As Mark Stoler has written: "The meeting had in effect determined future Allied strategy in Europe. As planned, Roosevelt had presented Stalin with all the alternatives. The Soviet leader had chosen OVERLORD on schedule with supporting action in Southern France, and the President had then backed him completely and further solidified the issue by linking it to the TRIDENT target date of May 1, 1944. Stalin's reinforcement consisted of his promise to enter the war against Japan as soon as Germany was defeated, a promise Roosevelt interpreted as a means of getting Washington to turn its undivided attention to OVERLORD."[39]

Most of the ensuing discussion at that Teheran meeting was devoted to Stalin's repeated efforts to pin down a firm date for the cross-Channel invasion and also an announcement of who would be the supreme commander of the operation and when exactly he would take charge. Stalin was particularly insistent about knowing how many divisions the Americans and British would take from Italy for ANVIL, the proposed southern France operation. Periodically Churchill would protest on this or that point, but without exception Roosevelt backed Stalin. Stalin was cruel, even mocking, to Churchill, and without protest from Roosevelt. At one point, taunting Churchill about his present counsel at Teheran to move slowly and carefully with OVERLORD, Stalin said: "In 1919 you were so keen to fight and now you don't seem to be at all. What happened? Is it advancing age? How many divisions do you have in contact with the enemy? What is happening to all those two million men you have in India?"[40]

Should Stalin's reference to 1919 elude the reader, it was the year in which the civil war in Russia was joined by Allied troops in strong opposition to Lenin and the Bolsheviks. Churchill had been one of the most ardent supporters of this opposition, repeatedly calling for more British troops and more funds for the defeat of the Bolsheviks, which he saw as absolutely vital to the stability of not only Europe but of the rest of the world.

Professor Kimball, editor of the *Correspondence,* offers an interesting sidelight on this. One day Mrs. Roosevelt put on the President's desk a paragraph she had taken from Churchill's *The World Crisis* which expressed eloquently Churchill's hatred of the Bolsheviks. Mrs. Roosevelt's pencilled comment was: "It is not surprising if Mr. Stalin is slow to forget."[41]

After Teheran, Churchill continued pushing his cause in his communications with the President. His advocacy went beyond the June 6 Normandy invasion and through much of July. Tirelessly he pointed out to the President that the Italian strategy was aimed first and foremost at the German troops. In a remarkable intercept, the British caught a secret message from Hitler to his commanding generals making it evident that nothing must be allowed to distract them from protection of Italy's northern border, with military divisions to be directed accordingly. Eisenhower himself, the Prime Minister reminded FDR, had in the beginning strongly opposed robbing the Italian campaign of vital divisions to be used in a merely auxiliary operation up the Rhône Valley in France. His own military chiefs, Churchill emphasized, were resolutely in favor of continuing the Italian strategy.

But Roosevelt was obdurate, almost serenely so, it would appear from his letters. Stalin had made his desires known at Teheran back in December 1943. "At Teheran we agreed on a definite plan of attack. That plan has gone well so far. Nothing has occurred to require any change." (June 29, 1944.)

In the first (and unsent) draft of an answering letter to Roosevelt, Churchill wrote in almost anguished tones: "The whole campaign in Italy is being ruined, and ruined for what? Simply for the amount of damage that 10 divisions, many quite unproved, the French almost entirely black and headed by inexperienced Commanders can do advancing up the Rhone valley about five months hence . . . no one ever contemplated that everything that was hopeful in the Mediterranean should be flung to one side, like the rind of an orange in order that some benefice might come to help the theatre of your command. . . . There is nothing I will not do to end this deadlock except become responsible for an absolutely perverse strategy. If you wish I will come at once across the ocean, to Bermuda, or Quebec, or, if you like, Washington. . . . But to agree to the whole great Mediterranean scene, with all its possibilities, being incontinently cast into ruin without any proportionate advantage gained by OVERLORD, that I cannot stand. I may add that I am supported by the War Cabinet and the British Chiefs of Staff. Therefore I think I have a right to some consideration from you, my friend, at a time when our joint ventures have dazzled the world with success." (June 30, 1944.)

Associates persuaded Churchill to tone down the emotional urgency of the draft. But the letter he actually sent on July 1 was hardly less poignant and it was more sharply, even devastatingly, composed. "What can I do, Mr. President," wrote Churchill toward the end of his letter, "when your Chiefs of Staff insist upon casting aside our Italian offensive campaign, with all its dazzling possibilities, relieving Hitler of all his anxieties in the Po Basin . . . and when we see the integral life of this campaign drained off into the Rhone Valley in the belief that it will in several months carry effective help to Eisenhower so far away in the north?"

Churchill apparently was very close to resignation as Prime Minister over his disappointment, even bitterness, in the President's repudiation of the Mediterranean-Italian peninsula strategy of meeting the Germans— and the Russians—in central Europe. General Brooke's diaries contain the following about the British chiefs and their meeting with Churchill. "I thought at first we might have trouble with him; he looked like wanting to fight the President. However in the end we got him to agree with our outlook, which is: 'All right, if you insist on being damned fools, sooner than fall out with you, which would be fatal, we shall be damned fools with you, and we shall see that we perform the role of damned fools damned well.' "[42]

Churchill was not totally bereft of American support. General Mark Clark, ranking American commander in Italy, wrote after the war, in mingled sorrow and resentment: "A campaign that might have changed the whole history of relations between the Western world and the Soviet Union was permitted to fade away. . . . The weakening of the campaign in Italy in order to invade Southern France, instead of pushing on into the Balkans, was one of the outstanding mistakes of the war. . . . Stalin knew exactly what he wanted . . . and the thing he wanted most was to keep us out of the Balkans. . . . It is easy to see therefore why Stalin favored ANVIL at Teheran."[43]

But the President couldn't be diverted by anyone from his central objective which was that of winning Stalin's total confidence and good will for the remaking of the world once the war was over. Never mind, he could have said to himself, the possible truth and present pertinence of Churchill's proposed strategy. The overriding truth is that Churchill is an imperialist to the core of his being—which indeed Churchill was, unabashedly so—and could never understand how important it is for me, Roosevelt, to respect Stalin's wishes and views wherever possible because of the need of the U.S. and the U.S.S.R. to cooperate in the postwar world to wipe out imperialism, colonialism, and other forces antagonistic to democracy.

Churchill's view of the importance of the Italian campaign was proved correct at the end of the war when the Germans began surrendering. In Italy just under one million German soldiers laid down their arms, proof positive of the correctness of the British position in 1944 that full prosecution of the Italian campaign would divert German forces from fighting either Eisenhower's advancing armies in the West or Stalin's in the East. "The surrender," a triumphant Churchill told the House of Commons on May 2, "included the Austrian provinces of Salzburg, Worarlberg, and the Tyrol, as well as portions of Carinthia and Styria." Roosevelt, alas, had been dead almost a month when these happy tidings were announced. Churchill was fully entitled to his triumph. He told the House of how "particularly difficult and depressing" it was for the army in Italy to have had "tremendous inroads" made upon it for "other great operations." Yet, "so weakened" as the Anglo-American armies in Italy were, they had made a decisive attack on the German soldiers; and now, Churchill continued, the number of Germans who surrendered to these Allied armies, "constitutes, I believe, a record in the whole of this war, and cannot fail to be helpful to further events, to which we are all looking forward."[44]

Even if FDR had been alive to hear Churchill's triumphant remarks, and felt obliged to concede, he could still have rejoiced in the thought that the real objective in his crippling of the Allied forces in Italy was not and had never been, what it would do to the Germans; but rather what it would do for the Soviets when the war was ended.

Martin Gilbert notes Churchill's reaction on the evening before his address to the House of Commons to the radio news from Hamburg that Hitler had died. "He had died" said the broadcast, "fighting with his last breath against Bolshevism." "Well," commented Churchill, "I must say, he was perfectly right to die like that." But Hitler did not so die; he committed suicide, with what final thoughts one can only guess.

CHAPTER THREE

"Stalin Is Not an Imperialist"

Roosevelt's courtship of Stalin proceeded apace at Yalta. Of all the episodes of the Second World War, the Yalta summit in early February 1945 probably has the worst odor. Some of the odor is deserved; some is not. Churchill said that if ten years had been taken in search for a meeting place, nothing worse than Yalta could conceivably have been found. Extremely difficult and exhausting to get to, with quarters congested and cramped, with the NKVD to be seen everywhere, with military guards with their rifles almost constantly at the ready, it was as though Stalin were torturing his allies into quick submission at the conference tables.

There are two main misconceptions of Yalta, both prominent even today. The first concerns the subjugation of eastern European states by the Soviets; the second centers on FDR's lavish gifts of Far Eastern lands and properties to Stalin.

It is not true that Yalta gave Stalin authority to subjugate the Baltics, Balkans, and large parts of Poland and eastern Europe. Yalta couldn't have given this permission to the Soviets, for they already had these countries in their possession when the Yalta summit began. The Soviets had taken, and they held, these countries by military force. If we want a correct source for the Soviet conquests of 1944, it is the Teheran summit. There, in late November 1943, Roosevelt had effectively given Stalin, in their private conversations, followed by plenary session ratifications, all necessary acquiescence in advance of Stalin's principal desires. Roosevelt's assurances were crucial because they made territorial bargaining, which Churchill wanted to pursue, impossible. The same held with respect to the Far East. Roosevelt at Teheran had assured Stalin of prizes in Asia if Stalin would but enter the war against Japan once Hitler had been defeated, indeed, as it came out at Yalta, Stalin only had to *agree* to join the Japanese war, he did not actually have to fight in it to win Roosevelt's concessions.

Second, it is false to charge General Marshall and the other Joint Chiefs with the pressure—for strictly military-strategic reasons—on the President that led to his Yalta actions. It has been widely argued that the Joint Chiefs were so apprehensive about the cost of defeating Japan that in order to be assured of Soviet help they recommended prizes of almost any magnitude to the Soviets. But as Marshall's biographer, Forrest C. Pogue, has pointed out persuasively, in documented detail, the truth is in the opposite corner. The American chiefs had become increasingly influenced by dispatches from General Deane, chief of the American Military Mission in Moscow, attesting to the license and outright corruption of the Russians with regard to lend-lease and in their whole attitude to the United States and Great Britain. Like Bullitt two years earlier, General Deane recommended strong use of the carrot-and-stick technique. So did Ambassador Harriman. And so did Secretary Stimson and General Marshall during the weeks before Yalta. But to no avail; Roosevelt paid no more heed to them than he had Bullitt. As Pogue writes: "The President handled the matter as if it were completely settled. Blandly, he wired Moscow that he had never doubted Stalin's intentions since the agreements were made concerning the Far East at Teheran; a week later he assured the Russian leader that he accepted his statement that he wanted to assist."[1]

I have just stressed that Yalta is not the source of the Soviet possessions in eastern Europe; that Teheran is. But Yalta performed a service to the Soviets that was almost as important to Stalin as the occupied areas themselves. This was the invaluable service of giving *moral legitimation* to what Stalin had acquired by sheer force. The Declaration on Liberated

Europe alone accomplished that. Such approbation, such moral license, could hardly have been anticipated by Stalin. But it was his all the same. As Chester Wilmot wrote in his *The Struggle for Europe,* "the real issue was not what Stalin would or could have taken but what he was given the right to do."[2]

As Wilmot and then a succession of other scholars pointed out, not only did power over the Baltic and Balkan peoples pass to Stalin; these peoples had to watch what democracy and freedom they had known before the war disappear, and then suffer the added humiliation of seeing such words as "free elections," "sovereignty," "democracy," "independence," and "liberation" deliberately corrupted, debased, made duplicitous, in the Declaration on Liberated Europe, the very title of which, given the ugly reality underneath, was a piece of calculated Soviet effrontery—one, however, that both Churchill and Roosevelt acquiesced in. Timothy Garton Ash has correctly written of the Declaration and the peoples it purported to represent:

> The peoples of "liberated" East Central Europe were not merely to be compelled to abandon their hopes of Democracy, Sovereignty, Independence, Representative Government—to use Churchill's own list. No, in accordance with the solemn terms of the Declaration on Liberated Europe they were to be compelled to abandon their hopes of Democracy *in the name of Democracy;* to lose Sovereignty and Independence in the name of Sovereignty and Independence; to see a mockery made of Representative Government in the name of Representative Government.
>
> Churchill himself recognized within a very few weeks after Yalta that the language of this "fraudulent document" was a useless weapon in the hands of the West. In fact, as Stalin doubtless understood, it was a powerful weapon added to the Soviet political armory. This is why the Soviet Union has ever since constantly referred to "Yalta" to legitimate its domination over East Central Europe.[3]

It is not only official Soviet Russia that speaks of the Yalta Conference and the Declaration on Liberated Europe in these terms. So do Soviet historians and political scientists. In this they differ sharply from Western, and especially American, scholars. The latter are today prone to declare the Yalta meeting of little or no importance inasmuch as the Red Army had already taken and claimed Poland and the eastern European countries. They agree generally that therefore Yalta is not the cause of the division, the partition of Europe. In this the Soviet scholars are ahead of their Western counterparts. For they know that while Stalin had already secured Poland and eastern Europe to Soviet suzerainty before Yalta, the endorsement, the legitimation, of these power grabs was as vital in the long run before the world as was the prior act of subjugation by force. In sum, Yalta is, as the Soviets declare, and have declared steadily since that summit, the effective cause of the partition.

No political language, and certainly not that in the Declaration on Liberated Europe, is any better or stronger than the interpretation the supreme power involved chooses to put on it. Since Lenin, the Soviet understanding of such Western words as "democracy," "liberation," "freedom," and "representation" has been a universe apart from the Western understanding. Had Roosevelt deigned to take with him to Yalta such genuine experts on the Soviet Union as Kennan, Loy Henderson, and Bullitt, he would surely have been cautioned about this. But he had not invited them. He didn't need them. Roosevelt had never paid any attention to their warnings and he paid no attention to the warnings he was beginning to get from Harriman in his ambassadorship at Moscow. When the Yalta conference was over and the Declaration on Liberated Europe signed by all three parties, Admiral Leahy voiced his doubts about any document such as the Declaration that permitted the Soviets such complete and autonomous interpretation. Roosevelt is said to have replied: "I know it, but it was the best I could get." If that is all FDR said, he was being disingenuous. On the basis of his record at Teheran and after, it was also pretty much all that he cared to get.

While Roosevelt felt obliged at one of Yalta's plenary sessions to support Churchill in postponing the acceptance that Stalin wanted immediately of the Soviet-sponsored Lublin government of Poland, he lost no time that very evening in writing a letter to Stalin in which he effectively renounced the position he had taken that afternoon. He wrote: "I am determined that there shall be no breach between ourselves and the Soviet Union. Surely there is a way to reconcile our differences." Then, as though to make doubly certain that his intent would not be lost on Stalin, the President wrote just below: "The United States will never lend its support in any way to any provisional government in Poland that would be inimical to your interests."[4]

What more was there to say? Stalin and Molotov had made clear beyond the slightest doubt that the official government of Poland, the government-in-exile in London, was unacceptable to them; it was, they repeatedly said, in league with the Nazis. The word Stalin and his Foreign

Minister used over and over about the official government was that it was "inimical" to the Soviets and could not, therefore be tolerated for a moment. Roosevelt's message told Stalin all he needed to know. There would be no further serious objection from the Anglo-American group about the Lublin government. Churchill might continue to object but, given the President's written sentiment that Stalin now had in hand, it would do no good.

There were other American contributions to Soviet peace of mind during the Yalta conference. Roosevelt assured Stalin that all American troops would be out of Europe less than two years after the German surrender; he suggested to Stalin that the two of them get together sometime to discuss the future of Hong Kong (Churchill was present when he said this), and as recorded in the diary of General Brooke, he said: "Of one thing I am certain, Stalin is not an imperialist."[5]

More important was the President's support of Stalin's position on France. Roosevelt knew that the postwar status of France was second only in Stalin's mind to the status of Germany. Repeatedly he told Roosevelt that France did not deserve to be a first class power; it must be stripped of overseas possessions and reduced to third class status in western Europe. The reason is clear. Stalin did not want *any* first rate national power between him and the English Channel. Roosevelt agreed with him until the final hours of the Yalta conference. At Yalta, in a private meeting with Stalin, Roosevelt said he "would now tell the Marshal something indiscreet, since he would not wish to say it in front of Prime Minister Churchill, namely that the British for two years have had the idea of artificially building up France into a strong power."[6]

Roosevelt agreed with Stalin that even to allow France a share of the military occupation of Germany was unwise but could be tolerated as "a kindness" as long as France wasn't allowed to participate in the control machinery.

Predictably, the minutes of the plenary session following the private conversation read: "The President said he favored the French request for a zone, but that he agreed with Marshal Stalin that France should not take part in the control machinery, otherwise other nations would demand participation."[7]

Churchill had, also predictably, a sharply different attitude toward France and her rehabilitation into a major power. He pointed out "that every nation had had their difficulties in the beginning of the war and had made mistakes. . . . While it was true that France had not been much help in the war, she still remained the nearest neighbor of Germany and of great importance to Great Britain. . . . He concluded by saying that we must provide for France in the future to stand guard on the left hand of Germany otherwise Great Britain might again be confronted with the specter of Germany on the Channel at the Channel ports."[8]

Or the Soviet Union! Naturally Churchill made no such reference, but it is hard to think that, after a quarter of a century of condemning Bolshevik Russia as a menace to the world, he did not have that country equally in mind along with Germany. At least equally. Churchill's view was that the greater danger in the long run could well be the Soviet Union, given its geopolitical position in the Eurasian Heartland, its powerful commitment to Communism as a potential world faith, and its mask, which Hitler's Nazi Germany had never succeeded in wearing, that led some to believe that behind Russian aggression lay a redemptive mission on behalf of the exploited and desperate masses. Given Germany's defeat, France was the only possible barrier to the Soviets overrunning western Europe.

In the end, Churchill managed to win at Yalta; not only with respect to a French zone in postwar Germany but even to a French position on the Control Commission. Roosevelt, for obvious reasons, came under heavy pressure from some of his own advisers to give up the attitude toward France he shared with Stalin—much as, earlier, he had been overruled by wise heads with respect to the pastoralization of Germany. But before Roosevelt voted with Churchill on the matter, he saw Stalin privately to inform him that he felt obliged to change his view. It is possible that even Hopkins saw the necessity of an American change of position on postwar France.

If Churchill is to be trusted, Roosevelt's faith in Stalin even reached the point where he expressed intent to share the secret of the atom bomb with the Soviet leader. In a minute to Eden on March 25—well before the Alamogordo test—Churchill wrote: "I was shocked at Yalta too when the President in a casual manner spoke of revealing the secret to Stalin, on the grounds that de Gaulle, if he heard of it, would certainly double-cross us with Russia." He added: "My agreement with President Roosevelt in writing forbids either party to reveal to anyone else the secret. . . ."[9]

Whether Roosevelt did impart to Stalin the secret is not known. Probably not. Interestingly, when President Truman informed Stalin about it at Potsdam in July 1945—at Joseph E. Davies's strong request, in order to cheer up Stalin—he seemed to show little surprise or interest. It is less likely that this reaction came from Roosevelt having possibly told him at Yalta than from his knowledge of the heavy yield in atom bomb secrets from the Rosenbergs, Fuchs, and others during the course of the war. Very probably he knew a good deal more about the bomb than Truman, who had been kept in the dark by Roosevelt about most things pertaining to the war.

Roosevelt was at his most generous at Yalta during the session on the rewards, territorial and other, to which the Soviets would be entitled for joining the war in the Pacific after the defeat of Hitler. Churchill chose not to attend. The meeting between Roosevelt and Stalin was under strictest secrecy, as were the minutes afterward. More than a month passed before Churchill received his copy, and when he read them, he instructed Eden to put them under lock and key.

Roosevelt didn't demur at a single request or suggestion from Stalin.[10] Stalin received almost immediately the southern half of Sakhalin Island, the Kurile Islands, and a warm water port at the end of the South Manchurian railway at Dairen on the Kwantung Peninsula. Roosevelt admitted on the last that he hadn't yet had time to consult Chiang Kai-shek on the matter, but he would and he believed there would be no difficulty. He said also that he hoped the British would give up Hong Kong to the Chinese.

This was just the beginning of the Roosevelt-Stalin feast. Stalin took pains to make clear that he would have the difficult task of "reporting" whatever he did here to the Russian people. They would be unhappy with him, he continued, at the thought of another war hard on the heels of the Great Patriotic War unless he could assure them positively that there would be substantial compensation for the Soviet Union in territory and suzerainty. Stalin pointed out that the Russian people would be hard to convince, because Japan was a country "with which they had no great trouble."

The gods in heaven must have dissolved in laughter at the thought of a concerned, worried Stalin "reporting" to his people in order to have their consent. But the farce continued in all solemnity. "Stalin insisted that these agreements [on Far Eastern gifts and concessions to the Soviets] must be put in writing and must contain the statement: 'The Heads of the Three Great Powers have agreed that these claims of the Soviet Union shall be unquestionably fulfilled after Japan has been defeated.' "[11]

Since some of the territory Roosevelt was giving to Stalin belonged to

the Republic of China, Stalin inquired whether the President had had an
opportunity to discuss and clear this with Chiang Kai-shek.

> The President replied that he had not had an opportunity to talk to Marshal
> Chiang Kai-shek, and he felt that one of the difficulties of speaking to the
> Chinese was that anything said to them was known to the whole world in
> twenty-four hours.
>
>   Marshal Stalin agreed and said he did not think it was necessary yet to
> speak to the Chinese and that he could guarantee the security of the
> Supreme Soviet. He added that it would be well to leave here with these
> conditions set forth in writing agreed to by the three powers.
>
>   The President indicated that he thought this could be done.

Understandably Stalin wanted that agreement in writing, signed by
Churchill and Roosevelt as well as himself. No one could be absolutely
certain of the length of the Pacific war—after all, Japan might surrender
before long—and Stalin didn't want to be hurried once Germany had
been destroyed. What was important, what was vital, was getting written
agreement from Britain and America that come what may respecting the
war with Japan, the Soviet Union was entitled to these immensely valuable concessions in the Far East simply by virtue of entering into the
agreement at Yalta.

Stalin asked if Roosevelt planned to base American troops in Korea;
Roosevelt assured him he did not. Marshal Stalin said that the Chinese
"needed some new leaders around Chiang Kai-shek." The President said
the fault lay more with the Kuomintang than with the "so called communists." There was complete agreement on the desirability of trusteeships
for Pacific islands after the war, something Churchill abominated. Finally,
Roosevelt assured Stalin that the status of Outer Mongolia would be
secured for the Soviets. Of course it was not the Soviets's fault that the
American atom bomb ended the Pacific war before Stalin could send so
much as a platoon to participate in the invasion of Japan. But then it wasn't
Stalin's fault either that so handsome a smorgasbord of territorial delights
in the Asian Pacific wound up in Soviet hands. The President had charm-
ingly proffered them or had in other ways made it clear that they all
belonged to the Russian people.

Ambassador Harriman, who had made every effort to warn Roosevelt
about Stalin's territorial hunger before this session, did not like the
concessions that had been made and spoke again to Roosevelt after the
meeting; again to no avail. He took copies of the documents to the

American chiefs, hoping that in the interest of sheer military strategy they would object; but they didn't. They doubtless agreed wholeheartedly with the President's generosity. [12] They knew very well indeed the President's warmth toward Stalin and the Soviets and his dream of working with Stalin after the war for a world of peace and democracy. And they doubtless agreed with that too.

It would be sad to end this part of the chapter without citing a memorandum that Hopkins wrote and passed over to the President during a final session at Yalta. An altercation among the three powers arose concerning German reparations. Pressure seemed to be growing on Stalin to join Churchill and Roosevelt on a point. Hopkins wrote (the memorandum is reprinted in facsimile in Sherwood's *Roosevelt and Hopkins* on page 860) to FDR: "The Russians have given us so much at this conference that I don't think we should let them down. Let the British disagree if they want to, and continue their disagreement at Moscow." And that, it will come as no surprise to the reader to learn, is exactly how it all ended.

We come now to the post-Yalta events in eastern Europe instigated by Stalin. More to the point here, we come also to the extreme differences in the reactions between Churchill and Roosevelt regarding these events. In their immediate reports to Congress, Parliament, and the press after their return from the Yalta conference, there was not much difference between Roosevelt and Churchill. Roosevelt reported that he and "Mr. Stalin" were alike "realists," and that it was in these terms that he looked forward to long cooperation between the U.S. and the U.S.S.R. in the postwar world. Churchill told the House of Commons that "Marshal Stalin and the Soviet leaders wish to live in honorable friendship and equality with the Western democracies." He added that he "felt that their word was their bond." Churchill told intimates that he had in all truth been impressed by Stalin's scrupulous observance of his word to Churchill that he would not interfere in Greece at the time of the Christmas crisis in 1944.

But by early March, Churchill was beginning to voice his alarm about the actions of the Soviets in Poland, Rumania, and elsewhere in eastern Europe. The sham of the Soviet backed Lublin government of Poland was revealed early.

Protests by Harriman and his British counterpart in Moscow were ignored, possibly laughed at, by Stalin and Molotov. After all, they had in the form of the Declaration on Liberated Europe all the grounds they needed for defending and rationalizing their brutal acts against the Poles.

Such matters as free elections, democracy, independence, fair representation, and the like had been specifically entrusted to the occupying power in all the "liberated" states of Europe.[13] The fact that Stalin and Molotov had different definitions for democracy and free elections than Churchill and Roosevelt was irrelevant and inconsequential.

From Moscow, Ambassador Harriman cabled Roosevelt: "Unless we take issue with present policy, there is every indication that the Soviet Union will become a world bully."[14] General Deane, head of the American military commission in Moscow, sent almost identical warnings to the White House. But the sharpest and most detailed warnings to the President were from Churchill, beginning in early March and continuing until Roosevelt's death on April 12.

On March 6, messages reached Churchill from his ambassador in Moscow about the mass arrests taking place in Cracow, with whole trainloads of Polish intellectuals, priests, professors, and labor union leaders being taken to a huge prison-work camp in Voroshilovgrad. As many as 6,000 former Home Army officers were put in a camp near Lublin, overseen and directed by Soviet officials indifferent to the publicity. The news from other parts of Europe, including the Baltic States and Rumania, was no better. All the rhetoric of democracy and liberty and representation notwithstanding, the process of sovietization was under way. The bitterness of the fruit of Yalta and the Declaration on Liberated Europe was beginning to be plain to the world.

On March 8, Churchill wrote a long letter to Roosevelt, apprizing him of the full, sordid picture in eastern Europe and particularly the cruel joke perpetrated upon the Poles in the name of "free" and "democratic" elections. He emphasized that nothing short of the two of them taking the matter straight to Stalin had the slightest chance of redirecting Soviet activities in Rumania and Poland. But Roosevelt would not join Churchill in signing a letter of protest. It would be much better, Roosevelt said, for the two of them to stay out of it and allow their ambassadors to seek a "truce" in Poland. "I feel that our personal intervention would best be withheld until every other possibility of bringing the Soviet Union into line has been exhausted. I very much hope, therefore, that you will not send any message to Uncle Joe at this juncture—especially as I feel that certain parts of your proposed text might produce a reaction quite contrary to your intent." (March 11, 1945.)

To which Churchill replied: "I wonder which you have in mind. We might be able to improve the wording. But I am convinced that unless we can induce the Russians to agree to these fundamental points of procedure, all our work at Yalta will be in vain." Then Churchill came to the heart of his reply to the lame and evasive response that had come over Roosevelt's name.

> I do not wish to reveal a divergence between the British and the United States governments, but it would certainly be necessary for me to make it clear that we are in the presence of a great failure and an utter breakdown of what was settled at Yalta, but that we British have not the necessary strength to carry the matter further and that the limits of our capacity to act have been reached.
>
> The moment that Molotov sees that he has beaten us away from the whole process of consultations among Poles to form a new government, he will know that we will put up with anything. (March 13.)

The reply to this from the White House manifested, or at least pretended to manifest, indignation that Churchill should think there was a "divergence" between Britain and the U.S. "From our side there is certainly no evidence of any divergence of policy. We have merely been discussing the most effective tactics, and I cannot agree with you that we are confronted with a breakdown of the Yalta agreement. . . ." (March 15.)

The differences between Roosevelt and Churchill were large and becoming larger by the day. Roosevelt could not bring himself to seem to be opposing and distrusting Stalin. He thus counselled and recounselled patience, inaction, trust, and respect toward Stalin.

Matters became relentlessly worse as Stalin widened and intensified his programs of terror, execution, and imprisonment in the Soviet-occupied sections of Europe. Churchill had proposed at Yalta that a very high-level international commission supervise the Polish elections coming up in a matter of weeks. But Roosevelt objected immediately—saving Stalin the necessity—on the ground that "low level" observers were sufficient. Now in late March, in the light of Soviet depredations in Poland, Churchill proposed again putting the elections under a high international commission. Once again Roosevelt demurred.

Only once during the spring of 1945 did FDR take sharp, even bitter, exception to a message from Stalin to both Churchill and himself. Stalin, in words of unsurpassed ugliness in World War II, accused the two leaders of having had exploratory talks behind his back with the Germans in Berne, Switzerland. What actually happened there was an agreement by Allen Dulles of the OSS to meet informally with a German general about *the possibility of surrender of the German armies in Italy* to the western Allies. Dulles acted solely on his own, stressing the necessarily informal, unbinding nature of the confidential talks; there were no Soviet troops fighting in Italy in any event. Stalin, however, reacted like a struck rattlesnake. His communication to Roosevelt and Churchill was, Ambassador Harriman later wrote, "the most bitter and the most insulting I had seen. It went beyond anything he had sent before. And it jarred Roosevelt into recognizing that the postwar period was going to be less pleasant than he had imagined. The President was deeply hurt."[15]

The President was indeed! The response that he sent to Stalin (first in the form of a draft for Churchill to read and approve) was, as were all of Roosevelt's important messages to Churchill, drafted by members of his staff, but it is more than merely possible that the final sentence was conceived and written by President Roosevelt. After a detailed refutation of Stalin's charges, Roosevelt wrote, to conclude his letter: "Frankly, I cannot avoid a feeling of bitter resentment toward your informers, whoever they are, for such vile representations of my actions or those of trusted subordinates."[16]

It is hard not to see those final words of FDR's letter as anything but the deeply grieved and torn sentiments of the lover betrayed. For without doubt Franklin Roosevelt had spent the war giving everything to Stalin and asking nothing in return. And now this! But FDR's equanimity was quickly restored. He lost little time in writing Stalin, referring to Berne as a "minor" affair. Harriman tried hard to persuade the President to drop the word "minor," but Roosevelt refused, insisting that the whole shocking affair was insignificant.

Churchill did not take Stalin's communication so lightly, but there was nothing he could do beyond muttering that Stalin's message of asserted "apology" was anything but that. Churchill continued through March and April of 1945 to seek to stimulate Roosevelt to join him in direct approaches to Stalin regarding the reports from Poland, Rumania, and other countries. On April 5, Churchill wrote to FDR: "We must always be anxious lest the brutality of the Russian messages does not foreshadow some deep change of policy for which they are preparing. On the whole I incline to think it is no more than their natural expression when vexed or anxious. For that very reason I deem it of the highest importance that a firm and blunt stand should be made at this juncture by our two countries. . . . I believe this is the best chance of saving the future. If they are ever convinced that we are afraid of them and can be bullied into submission, then indeed I should despair of our future relations with them and much else."

At the same time that Roosevelt was receiving such counsel and foreboding from Churchill, he was also receiving it from his ambassador in Moscow, Averell Harriman. In a March 21 message that he held until he could carry it personally to the President, he wrote: "I feel the time has come to reorient our whole attitude, and our method of dealing with the Soviet government. Unless we wish to accept the 20th century barbarian invasion, with repercussions extending further and further, and in the East as well, we must find ways of arresting the Soviet domineering policy." In a separate message, Harriman wrote: "We must come to clearly realize that the Soviet program is the establishment of totalitarianism, ending personal liberty and democracy as we know it."[17]

On March 24, Harriman, outraged by Soviet brutality and callousness toward American prisoners-of-war rescued from German prison camps, begged the President to communicate directly with Stalin as a means of bringing the mistreatment to immediate stop. "It was preposterous," Harriman added, "for Stalin to argue that the Red Army command could not be bothered with perhaps a dozen American officers in light of all the help the United States had sent to Russia over the war years." He urged the President to cable Stalin once again and to consider retaliatory steps, for example by instructing Eisenhower to limit the movements of Russian contact officers in France. But Roosevelt had decided against further personal appeals. In a message to Harriman, dated March 26, he replied: "It does not appear appropriate for me to send another message now to Stalin. . . ."[18]

On April 2, Harriman cabled the President a message similar to Churchill's: "I feel certain that unless we do take action in cases of this kind, the Soviet government will become convinced that they can force us to accept any of their decisions on all matters and it will be increasingly difficult to stop their aggressive policy."[19]

Apparently Harriman did have occasional effect on FDR's feelings. One day at lunch with an old friend, Anna Rosenberg Hoffman, Roosevelt received an urgent cable from Harriman that so incensed him he banged the arms of his wheel chair, saying: "Averell is right. We can't do business with Stalin. He has broken every one of the promises he made at Yalta."[20] About the same time he made a similar remark to Anne O'Hare McCormick of The New York Times. The President continued to believe in the

Yalta agreements, but he felt that Stalin "was no longer a man of his word; either that or he was no longer in control of the Soviet government."[21]

There is also the letter for Roosevelt's signature prepared on April 6, when the President was in Warm Springs. His aide Admiral Leahy was the draftsman. Leahy had been increasingly persuaded by Harriman's and Deane's urgent cables from Moscow of the drift of Stalin's attitude toward eastern Europe and of the necessity of the U.S. joining Churchill in a stronger stance. What Leahy wrote for Roosevelt's signature to be transmitted to Churchill was:

> I am pleased with your very clear strong message to Stalin.
>
> We must not permit anybody to entertain a false impression that we are afraid.
>
> Our armies will in a very few days be in a position that will permit us to become "tougher" than has heretofore appeared advantageous to the war effort.

There are some scholars and journalists who have taken this reply to Churchill to signify a late conversion to a realistic, proper assessment of Stalin. I incline, however, to the view expressed by Professor Kimball, editor of the *Correspondence*. Kimball observes that Leahy's draft from Washington was received and signed by Roosevelt in Warm Springs and returned to Washington, all within one hour and twenty-eight minutes. This was, Kimball writes, "hardly time for Roosevelt to have reconsidered and redirected the entire thrust of the wartime and postwar policy toward the Soviet Union. In fact, one wonders if the President gave this message any consideration at all, particularly in view of his poor health."[22]

No doubt this quickly read and returned draft of a letter to Churchill is sincere, as no doubt his complaints about Stalin's behavior uttered to Anna Rosenberg Hoffman and Anne O'Hare McCormick are entitled to be accepted as sincere. But they can be perfectly sincere in the moment's expression and yet be unrepresentative of his complete, considered thought. FDR had endured with seeming composure harsh actions by Stalin toward him and the Anglo-American cause. It is hard to believe that Roosevelt, having spent the war in calculated courtship of Stalin for his postwar uses, would now, this late in the war, jettison strong convictions of four years's standing.

A truer measure of Roosevelt's feelings in early April 1945 lies in the last messages he sent to Churchill, Harriman, and Stalin from Warm Springs the day before he died on April 12. To Churchill he wrote: "I would minimize the general Soviet problem as much as possible because these problems in one form or other seem to arise every day and most of them straighten out as in the case of the Berne meeting. . . ." To these words to Churchill the President added somewhat cryptically: "We must be firm, however, and our course thus far is correct." These words were written in Roosevelt's own hand. So were his final words to Harriman: "It is my desire to consider the Berne misunderstanding a minor incident." And in his letter to Stalin, FDR thanked him for his "fresh explanation of the Soviet point of view on the Berne incident which it now appears has faded into the past without having accomplished any useful purposes."[23]

No one can know for sure in such matters. Perhaps after a message of this gentleness to Stalin—strenuously engaged at that very moment in the cynical betrayal of every hope aroused in the West by the Yalta conference—FDR would have quickly turned himself to a Churchillian view of the Soviet Union. Perhaps. But such a conversion strikes one as highly implausible. And, as I have noted above, Harriman himself said that he had found "no persuasive evidence" of such a transformation of Roosevelt's views of Stalin and the Soviets.

POSTSCRIPT:

From Yalta to Berlin

At one of the private meetings between Stalin and Roosevelt at Yalta, the President, apropos of nothing thus far said in the conversation, told Stalin that bets had been made aboard the cruiser that brought the Americans over "as to whether the Russians would get to Berlin before the Americans got to Manila." The transcript continues: "Marshal Stalin remarked that he was certain that the Americans would get to Manila before the Russians got to Berlin since there was at present very hard fighting going on at the Oder line." Curiously, Roosevelt left unspoken the fact that a competition worth betting on was gradually building up between the Russians and the Anglo-Americans in Europe, with specific reference to Berlin. It was as though he was consigning Berlin to Stalin.

A few minutes later, Roosevelt volunteered another opinion that could not have failed to get Stalin's attention. "The President said he felt that the armies were getting close enough to have contact between them and he hoped General Eisenhower would communicate directly with the Soviet Staff rather than through the Chiefs of Staff in London and in Washington, as in the past."

"Marshal Stalin agreed and thought it was very important and promised that the staffs would work out the details of this suggestion."[24]

Stalin would have thought the President's idea even more important had he been able to look ahead about six weeks to the famous telegram Eisenhower dispatched directly to Stalin himself on March 28. The substance of the telegram was a candid outline of the strategy Eisenhower would pursue during the remaining weeks of the war in Europe. The strategy involved a major thrust to the south, toward Dresden and the mountainous area beyond. But what was important about the telegram was that it made no reference to taking and occupying Berlin. Berlin had been most definitely included in the Combined Chiefs's strategy that was unanimously approved at the beginning of February at their Malta meeting on the way to the Yalta summit.

Stalin's joy must have been intense. He knew very well the value of Berlin and the crucial importance of being first to reach the bunker that housed Hitler, Eva Braun, the Goebbels family, Martin Bormann, and other high, hated Nazi principals. The Soviet capture of Berlin, courtesy of General Eisenhower, would be a crowning completion to a larger Soviet plan to assume hegemony in all of central Europe—Vienna and Prague included. Stalin knew this; and he knew that Churchill had been working against its possibility from early in the war. Stalin must also have known that the estimable and personable General Eisenhower would never have taken it upon himself to dispatch a telegram effectively relinquishing Berlin without the certain knowledge that it fell clearly within an East-West policy that Roosevelt had cherished from the beginning. Stalin might well have considered it another generous gift from the President, in accord with their private discussion at Yalta.

Churchill and his chiefs knew nothing of the telegram until March 29, the day following its dispatch to Stalin, when information copies were received from SHAEF. The telegram was a double shock to Churchill and his chiefs. There was first the gift—the wanton gift in Churchill's mind—of Berlin to the Soviets. Second was the realization that Eisenhower, in perhaps the most unEisenhowerian act of his career, had ceded Berlin to Stalin without notifying, much less consulting, in advance the Combined

Chiefs to whom the Supreme Commander was responsible in military matters and had been since the creation of SHAEF.

Churchill employed all his arts to convince Eisenhower to retract the telegram, but Ike stubbornly insisted that he had, within the terms of his command, the right to make direct contact with Stalin, to make the decision unilaterally to remove Berlin from Allied objectives, and to do so without the approval of the Combined Chiefs. Moreover, he had the immediate endorsement of General Marshall, of the American chiefs of staff, and, he had every reason to believe, of the President.

Churchill fumed, and was aghast at the implications. The British chiefs were in full agreement that Berlin was a crucially important prize for both military and political reasons. Its capture was crucial in the war itself and in determining the postwar balance of power in Europe.

There are some who have said it was all supererogatory; that the Anglo-American troops couldn't have reached Berlin before the Soviets did, which turned out to be late April, as matters transpired. At the time of Ike's telegram to Stalin the Soviets were considerably closer to Berlin than were the western Allies. But German opposition to the Anglo-American forces was almost minimal compared to the depth and intensity of German resistance on the eastern front. The German people dreaded and feared the Russians. Their attitude toward the British and the Americans was substantially different.

The 9th U.S. Army under the command of Lt. General William Simpson, which was then a part of Montgomery's larger army group, reached the Elbe River on April 11. Beyond the Elbe was Berlin, about sixty miles distant. Two trial forays across the river were made successfully by the Americans. To General Simpson and to every eager soldier in his command, the way to Berlin and glory was wide open.

Jubilation became sheer depression when Simpson was ordered by General Bradley—to whose armies the U.S. 9th had just been transferred from Montgomery's command—to halt at the Elbe, to make no effort to cross the river unless and until specific orders were drawn up later. Simpson was crushed. So would be every soldier in his army. He asked for and got a meeting with General Bradley. Simpson asked who was ultimately responsible for halting of the 9th Army. Bradley replied "Eisenhower." That pretty much ended it. They both knew—who in high command didn't?—that Eisenhower never did anything of importance without clearing it with and getting the advice of General Marshall, whom Ike regarded very much as a father. There was also the fact that not once in his World War II career did Eisenhower ever deviate from the President's political policy regarding Stalin and the Soviets. He knew exactly what that policy was. Almost certainly Eisenhower had been informed by Marshall of the President's private agreement with Stalin respecting direct communication. Perhaps Bradley had also been informed to that effect by Eisenhower.

Our only certainty is that for Simpson, the war was, in all important emotional respects, over. We know that Ike's telegram remained for days the subject of strong difference of opinion between Churchill and Marshall, Churchill and Eisenhower, and Churchill and Roosevelt. Churchill wrote to Eisenhower—after Ike had tried to convince him that there was military advantage in *not* crossing the Elbe—the following:

> I do not know why it would be an advantage not to cross the Elbe. If the enemy's resistance should weaken, as you evidently expect and which may well be fulfilled, why should we not cross the Elbe and advance as far eastward as possible? This has an important political bearing, as the Russian armies of the South seem certain to enter Vienna and overrun Austria. If we deliberately leave Berlin to them, even if it should be in our grasp, the double event may strengthen their conviction, already apparent, that they have done everything. . . .
>
> I do not consider myself that Berlin has yet lost its military and certainly not its political significance. The fall of Berlin would have a profound psychological effect on German resistance in every part of the Reich. . . . The idea that the capture of Dresden and junction with the Russians there would be a superior gain does not commend itself to me. . . . While Berlin remains under the German flag, it cannot, in my opinion, fail to be the most decisive point in Germany.[25]

Let us, Churchill concluded his letter, continue the strategy that was ratified officially at Malta, the strategy "on which we cross the Rhine, namely that the 9th U.S. Army should march with the 21st Army Group to the Elbe and beyond Berlin."

Churchill wrote to Roosevelt, though he must have known that the letter would be useless.

> The Russian armies will no doubt overrun all Austria and enter Vienna. If they also take Berlin, will not their impression that they have been the overwhelming contributor to our common victory be unduly imprinted in

their minds, and may this not lead them into a mood which will raise grave and formidable difficulties in the future? I therefore consider that from a political standpoint we should march as far east into Germany as possible and that should Berlin be within our grasp we should certainly take it. This also appears sound on military grounds.

The reply sent in Roosevelt's name on April 4 is a model of the blandly evasive, ending, however, with "You have my assurance of every cooperation." Churchill, knowing that his cause was hopeless, ended the controversy by sending to the President a Latin quotation: *Amantium irae amoris integratio est.* Roosevelt's staff translated it as "Lovers' quarrels always go with true love," but Churchill translated it for his typist, as "The wrath of lovers hots up their love."

It can come as no surprise to learn that General Simpson never forgot an iota of the experience. It seems to have rankled in his mind to the end. In 1972, in a frank and detailed interview, Simpson said, among other things:

> I had six or seven divisions on the Elbe river there. . . . I had two army corps there and was in very good shape to have gone on and made the advance. . . . Harry Hopkins later made a statement that we'd outrun our supplies and all that sort of thing. Well, he didn't know what he was talking about because my army was in good shape, the supplies were in good shape, and we could have gone right on to Berlin and put up a darned good show. I had even railroads coming down into my area, carrying supplies. And I had these 10-ton truck companies, hundreds of them. . . . We had a bridgehead across there with one pontoon bridge across and another one to be built that night. . . . So I think we could have ploughed across there within twenty-four hours and been in Berlin in twenty-four to forty-eight hours easily.

General Simpson also stressed that the area between the Elbe and Berlin was lightly defended, "by a kind of crust of newly formed units that were putting up some opposition. . . . What was left of the German armies were over there against the Russians except this little crust that was around me, and a good part of that was pulled away about the time I was halted. And, I don't know, I have a feeling that maybe the Germans might have welcomed us. . . . They were in terrible shape, you know."[26]

There is no single episode in the history of the Second World War more fraught with subsequent controversy than the telegram that General Eisenhower sent unilaterally, without any known consultation or prior notification, to Stalin; the telegram that effectively disclaimed Anglo-American military interest in Berlin. Amidst all the controversy—which lasts down to the present moment without sign of early terminus—there is at least one conclusion drawn by all analysts and historians: The decision to send the telegram and to send it in the singular way in which Ike sent it to Stalin was, almost without question, a purely personal decision. If nothing else, the utter lack of prior notification or consultation attests to that fact.

The strictly personal cast of the telegram was mainifest too in the confusion it caused in the American Military Mission under General Deane in Moscow. Not even Ike's most adoring followers ever credited him with a gift for lucid and felicitous prose. Whether in speech or writing, his syntax could and often did become scrambled. This seems to have been the case with the telegram. Twenty-four hours were expended in a frantic effort by General Deane in Moscow to clear up the meaning of the telegram in order that it might be correctly translated into Russian for delivery to Stalin.

But if there is agreement among students on the personal character of Eisenhower's decision to communicate suddenly with Stalin, there is little if any consensus on the circumstances which came to a focus in his decision. What in the end was the chief inspiration of his personal decision? The range of suggested reasons—all speculative—is wide. Some have adduced the so-called "southern redoubt" that, according to SHAEF, was being formed in the mountains of southern Germany for a last, Wagnerian battle in which every German soldier would die for Hitler after having inflicted heavy casualties on Anglo-American and Russian forces. No one else, however, perceived such a redoubt building and even SHAEF dropped the myth before long. Churchill and his chiefs were disdainful from the start at the report.

Yet another reason advanced for Eisenhower's decision to bypass Berlin by sending most of his armies southward in the direction of Dresden, without ever crossing the Elbe, was a desire to make certain that the eastward advancing Anglo-Americans and the westward advancing Soviet armies didn't collide head-on, with possible dangerous friction. Churchill, Alanbrooke, and Montgomery were no more persuaded by this reason than by the myth of the redoubt. It was preposterous to suppose safeguards couldn't have been created to prevent a possible collision and still allow Montgomery's and Simpson's forces to Berlin.

Another, and possibly the most commonly adduced cause of the telegram to Stalin was Eisenhower's desire to please General Bradley whose American army group was poised for a southern advance, and who very much wanted to have Simpson's 9th U.S. Army back under his, rather than Montgomery's, command. Bradley had erred at the Ardennes setback in December and January, and Montgomery, who eventually was responsible for the repulse of the Germans, had dealt with Bradley in humiliating fashion. The desire for some kind of atonement was certainly present; Bradley naturally was very close to Eisenhower; they were often at each other's headquarters. Why not, then, pacify Bradley by giving back Simpson's American divisions to him and, in the process of robbing Montgomery, take Simpson away from the Elbe crossing and his long-planned dash to Berlin?

Suffice it to say that this explanation is no more credible than the others. As Alanbrooke and Montgomery agreed, everything of this sort could have been accomplished or rectified without necessarily sacrificing Berlin to the Russians, who did not reach Berlin until the very end of April, two weeks after Simpson's 9th U.S. Army would have almost certainly entered Berlin had it not been stopped cold at the Elbe by Eisenhower.

In a realm of speculation, one must offer his own particular surmise. Mine is that the seed of Eisenhower's bizarre decision on Berlin goes directly back to the *tête à tête* Stalin and Roosevelt had at Yalta. Certainly the question of why Eisenhower, six weeks later, violated the chain of command and ignored the Combined Chiefs, is given a reasonable answer. Roosevelt had suggested, with Stalin's immediate assent, that Eisenhower be licensed to do precisely what he wound up doing: that is, communicate with the Soviet High Command—which of course included Marshal Stalin—without feeling it necessary to go through cumbersome channels such as the Combined Chiefs. Although Eisenhower never referred to this license in his interchanges with Churchill and the British chiefs after the telegram had been sent, it was pure tact, certainly not ignorance, that impelled him to remain silent on the authority that Roosevelt, through Marshall, had given him.

At one point when the heat seemed to be rising ominously among the British leaders, Eisenhower cabled Marshall that if the Combined Chiefs ordered him to retract his order and to restore the objective of Berlin, he would. Marshall, who had given instant concurrence to Eisenhower's unilateral action, chose, however, to withhold the offer from the Combined Chiefs.

As the British sensed from the start, Eisenhower, no doubt somewhat conscience-stricken from his own unilateral communication with Stalin, made every effort to bury the significance of Berlin in a maze of other considerations. There was the alleged Nazi redoubt in the south; there was the necessity of transferring General Simpson and his 9th Army from Montgomery's group command back to Bradley's command; there was the fear of the Allied and Soviet armies colliding if both went to Berlin; and there was the need on personal grounds to restore Bradley's confidence in himself. Further, Bradley, on a quick estimate, foresaw the possibility of a hundred thousand Allied casualties if the road to Berlin were taken—an estimate ludicrously out of proportion with Lt. General Simpson's own on-the-spot view.

I will conclude this highly speculative matter with a personal anecdote. During the 1970s I became acquainted with a retired Lt. General who had served with SHAEF in the late phases of the war. Once, fresh from reading Cornelius Ryan's splendid treatment of the Eisenhower-commanded stop at the Elbe, I asked my friend what light he could throw on the matter. He smiled and said immediately: "George owed the President a good deal and knew it." So did Ike owe General Marshall a good deal. And the President? As we have seen, he liked gifts to Stalin: the perilous, suicidal convoys to Archangel and Murmansk in 1942; the fight for an immediate cross-Channel assault in the same year; the refusal to join Churchill in aiding the Polish Home Army in 1944; the gift of one third of the Italian navy; the acceptance of Lublin as Poland's government; the whole abandonment of the Mediterranean strategy anchored in Italy; and the proferring of Asiatic prizes for Stalin at Yalta. We can't be sure in such tenuous and controverted matters as Berlin, but it hardly taxes the imagination to suppose that this city was simply one more gift from the President, through high channels, to Stalin. FDR may well have thought to himself: with this final war gift, I will surely be able to handle Stalin in the postwar world.

CHAPTER
FOUR

"A New Period Has Opened"

There remains the question: What prompted Roosevelt as early as the summer of 1941 to commence his tireless, unrebuffable courtship of the totalitarian Stalin? It is easy to agree with George Kennan that "puerility" in the form of an arrant egotism and mindless complacency was the spur. No doubt. But that tells us nothing about the intellectual and political content of the puerility. Even when we are confronted by neurotics and psychotics in life there are intellectual patterns, however weird they might seem to us. The question becomes: What intellectual roots underlay the puerile courtship of a despot at least the equal of Hitler in the savageries committed during the 1930s?

The answer, in a word, is Wilsonianism. Roosevelt's mind was shaped—and in the process twisted—by one of the most powerful forces in American foreign policy since the Great War: Wilsonian idealism or moralism. It is likely that even if the young and ambitious Franklin Roosevelt hadn't served his idol as Assistant Secretary of the Navy, he would have become a Wilsonian. Young men of breeding and wealth who entered the private schools of the northeast and its ivy-league universities after about 1917 were prone to becoming Wilsonians. What better role model was there than this extraordinary man of moral fire, born a devout Calvinist, who would in his adolescence make the American nation the lasting object of his fire, who preached from the presidency of Princeton the message of service to country—"Princeton in the Nation's service"— and who tried every act by an iron morality rooted in Puritan New England, and who, in the climax of his life, led America into what had been nothing more than an imperialistic war, and who transformed it into a war to make the world safe for democracy? Add to those luminous career landmarks the Golgotha he went through as the result of a Judas, Senator Henry Cabot Lodge, and we have all the ingredients of sainthood as well as political leadership. To anyone who came of intellectual age in the 1920s, memory has to be deeply etched of Woodrow the Idealist, whose basic tragedy was that he came "twenty years before his time." Virtually every middle class to upper class home echoed this.

President Roosevelt wanted, in the depth of his soul, to succeed at the noble objective, the pursuit of which had cost Wilson his life, of making the world safe for democracy. How remarkable that he, Roosevelt, exactly twenty years after his idol's death should be in the post-Wilsonian role of leader of America in a second great opportunity to make the world safe for democracy. By 1944, Roosevelt had given the nation the New Deal, which he saw as a compassionate perfecting of the democracy Wilson had served. He had even climbed essentially the same prophetic steps which Wilson had climbed in the process of making up his mind about the wisdom and morality of taking America into the European war after it began in August 1914.

Wilson had been neutral during the first three years of the war; not simply neutral: passionately, dedicatedly neutral. "There is such a thing as a man being too proud to fight," he told his adoring followers at a Philadelphia rally on 10 May 1915. "We have stood apart, studiously neutral," he declared to Congress a year and a half later. But by February 1917 he had reached the point of "armed neutrality," and a week or so later he lashed out at "a little group of willful men" that were making "the United States helpless and contemptible" by opposing intervention in the war. And on 2 April of the same year he declared, in a speech requesting a declaration of war on Germany, "The world must be made safe for democracy."

Roosevelt, with perhaps fewer pawings at the air and clutchings of the breast, followed this route in at least some measure. From the time he scuttled the World Economic Conference in London shortly after he took office for his first term in March 1933, Roosevelt manifested little real interest in European affairs. But by 1938, events were heating up, and Stalin, Hitler, and Mussolini were projecting themselves upon the world stage. Roosevelt had no alternative but to become interested. There was also the dismal fact that after the severe recession of late 1937, the American economy, the ministrations of the New Deal notwithstanding, had slipped back to 1932 harshness. He was by no means the first ruler in history to find his attention turning to the dogs of war in the wake of domestic failures; nor would he be the last. Naturally, from the very beginning, he took sides—as Wilson had not in the same phase of war (but who didn't take sides with villains on the scale of Mussolini and Hitler engaged in fighting the two greatest of the European democracies, France and England?). But at the time he inaugurated the historic secret correspondence with Churchill in September 1939, when Churchill was serving the Admiralty in Chamberlain's government, Roosevelt was still very much the neutralist in heart and mind. Churchill, like all the British, couldn't help praying fervently, deep in his soul, that America, through Franklin D. Roosevelt's good offices, could be persuaded, one way or the other, to join Britain in the war against Germany. There was America's gigantic productive power to begin with; that would help even if American engagement in the war were not total. And there was always too the tantalizing prospect of drawing sooner or later on America's potential military power—soldiers, ships, and planes.

Even if Churchill hadn't practiced his arts, it is entirely likely that FDR., along with a rising number of Americans, would have been converted into something of an interventionist simply by the spectacle of the Battle of Britain in late 1940 and early 1941. In January 1941, Roosevelt, in his State of the Nation Address before Congress, defined a just war as one in behalf of the Four Freedoms: freedom of speech and expression; freedom of worship; freedom from want; and freedom from fear. He would be obliged to drop two of these freedoms when the Soviet Union became, willy nilly, Britain's and then America's ally. Like Wilson, Roosevelt saw war in moral terms, not those of mere national interest. Also like Wilson, Roosevelt was determined that Britain's and France's imperialism should not keep America's purity from penetrating the swamp.

Roosevelt was like Wilson in another vital respect. Both were less interested in the war than in the postwar world. Wilson had agonizedly reached interventionism only when he came to realize that if he and America were to play the great role in postwar peacemaking, neutrality would not be enough; there had to be participation, even though he found it necessary to hold his nose. Roosevelt, disciple of his master, seems to have seen the matter the same way. Once he had defined the distant war as a war for freedom and for representative democracy in the world, it was inevitable that his interest in all-out participation would mount quickly.

There is no surprise, thus, in the historic meeting with Churchill—at FDR's invitation—in Argentia Bay, off Newfoundland in August 1941. Roosevelt had deliberately kept to himself, and to Sumner Welles who had drafted it, the Atlantic Charter he wished Churchill to join him in signing. The President shrewdly asked Churchill if he would write a further draft of the Charter, which Churchill did, radioing its contents back to his War Cabinet for their approval.

There could be no reference in the Charter to the Four Freedoms which Roosevelt earlier in the year had made the *raison d'être* of the Second World War. For, much to the shock and bitter disappointment of Stalin, Hitler had invaded Russia in June, thus making the Soviet Union, inescapably, a partner of Britain in the war against Nazi Germany. Even Roosevelt knew that it would be grotesque to pen a charter for the signature of Stalin as well as Churchill in which the freedom of speech and the freedom to worship were contained. As it happened, there was never again in the war any reference by Roosevelt to the Four Freedoms he had so cherished when he first announced them to Congress. As I noted early in the book, it was George Kennan who, on the very hour in which he heard of the German invasion of Russia from his post in the Berlin embassy, wrote to his superiors in the State Department of how fundamentally this invasion of Russia, and this inevitable linking of America and Britain with the totalitarian Soviets changed the moral character of the war.

It was, then, a perfect Wilsonian overture FDR made to Churchill at Argentia Bay, one that if accepted made sure the moral basis of a war that too many Americans still thought was imperialist in basic character, with America playing once again the role of catspaw for British interests. Following the successful Atlantic Charter meeting, with Churchill's, and, eventually, Molotov's signatures on the document, Roosevelt began his unbroken, relentless series of acts of favor to Stalin which have been the principal content of this book. From his press conference in late 1941 in which he declared that on reading the Soviet Constitution he had found a freedom of religion much like the American freedom of religion, all the way through the politics of the second front, through Teheran and Yalta, down to his final message to Stalin the day before he died at Warm Springs, the courtship of Marshal Stalin by President Roosevelt was firm and serious.

Once again, why? Sir John Wheeler-Bennett, distinguished diplomatic historian, has given us a succinct statement of the ultimate reason: "President Roosevelt's ambition was to establish the United Nations but to superimpose upon it an American-Soviet alliance which should dominate world affairs to the detriment of Britain and France, and to this end he made copious concessions to Marshal Stalin."[1]

But why not an alliance with Britain instead of totalitarian Russia, or at least an alliance of the Big Three? Here we come to the heart of the Roosevelt disposition of mind in World War II. It was to the Soviet Union only that Roosevelt made his overtures of friendship because Britain embodied the imperialism he and his revered master, Woodrow Wilson, hated unrelentingly. For Roosevelt, the real struggle democracy must wage is against, not totalitarianism, but imperialism. When Churchill heard that Chiang Kai-shek didn't want a trusteeship or any other Chinese control of a certain area near China, he exclaimed, "Nonsense," at which point Roosevelt chided him: "Winston, this is something you are not able to understand. You have 400 years of acquisitive instinct in your blood, and you just don't understand how a country might not want to acquire land somewhere if they can get it. A new period has opened up in the world's history, and you will have to adjust to it."[2]

Churchill was not one to be turned away easily from his British heritage. When he made his celebrated—or notorious—announcement—"I have not become the King's First Minister to preside over the liquidation of the British Empire"—he was speaking, Wilmot tells us, directly and specifically to Roosevelt.[3] For from early in their correspondence it was made very evident that the President deplored just about everything in the British imperial system. Parenthetically it should be observed that in this respect Roosevelt joined a very large majority of the American people. The greatest single domestic argument against American participation in the Second World War was that we would serve as a tool of Great Britain. When Germany declared war on America a few days after Pearl Harbor, the newspapers were filled with editorials cautioning America not to become vulnerable to the wiles of imperial Great Britain.

It was Roosevelt's apprehension concerning these self-same wiles that led him to oppose strongly, early in the war, any wartime decisions about territories newly annexed or detached from countries or about spheres of influence. Not long after the Soviets were dragged into the war by the German invasion, and the U.S. had become perforce an ally of both Russia and Britain, Stalin let Churchill know that he expected full approval for the Soviets's retention of all the territorial gains effected in his pact with Hitler. He wanted the large piece of Poland, the Baltic States, and everything else the pact had conferred on Russia. Churchill didn't say yes or no, but advised Stalin against bringing the matter up with Roosevelt.[4]

But at Teheran, Roosevelt conceded all of this to Stalin. He said almost nothing about the advantages of Stalin's waiting until after the war when they could all three sit down at the peace table; to Churchill, yes, repeatedly. But not Stalin. General Brooke spoke for the rest of the British, surely, when he said: "Roosevelt's philosophy of postponing all questions of sphere of influence until after the war seemed strangely porous when it was a Soviet grab for power that loomed up, and strangely stiff, even unyielding, when it was the British or some other monarchical power."

Sir Arthur Bryant, in *Triumph in the West,* paraphrasing Robert Sherwood's *Roosevelt and Hopkins,* wrote: "In his private talks with Stalin he [FDR] deliberately gave [Stalin] the impression that, with its egalitarianism and forward looking outlook, America was better able to understand Russian needs than the Conservative imperialist power."[5]

There is not the slightest ground for thinking FDR to be indulging here in a cynical power play. As a faithful apostle of Woodrow Wilson he believed that imperialism of the British-French kind was the greatest enemy of democracy. "Of one thing I am sure, Stalin is not an imperialist," he exclaimed at Yalta. He couldn't have missed the barbarism, the signs of despotism in almost everything the Soviet government did; he couldn't have been altogether blind to the Soviet past of genocide in the Ukraine, the Great Terror of the 1930s, and Stalin's repeated declaration during his pact with Hitler that World War II had been started, not by Nazi Germany but by England and France.

But if the President wasn't blind to these offenses, it has to be said that he had a very special way of assimilating them and arranging them in his mind and conscience. It will be remembered that he alone "found" freedom of religion in Russia and promptly called a press conference to announce it. He told his Secretary of Labor after returning from Teheran that there was a "mystical devotion" among the Soviet leaders to their people, a desire to do first for others and only then for themselves.

It is hard to avoid the conclusion that Roosevelt saw the Soviet Union, its record of terror and slaughter, its omnipresent dictatorship and despotism notwithstanding, as containing a greater promise of democracy and freedom in the long run than Great Britain. Somehow in Roosevelt's vision all the ugly was squeezed out and what was left was a system in Russia not extremely different from his own American New Deal. Stalin was perhaps uncouth at times, carried the blood of barbarians in his veins, but on the other hand, Roosevelt may have thought, the Soviet Union, with all warts conceded in advance, was still constitutionally pledged to its people to provide jobs, medical care, and welfare very much on the order of his own New Deal; more repressive, of course, in fact too repressive, but with a level of repression not of disqualifying importance. There was also the constitutional pledge to build a classless society, which meant the kind of egalitarianism perhaps that Americans had learned from Democratic Party populists. Also the Soviet Union was forward-looking, progressive in thrust, and the aged European imperial states were not.

Nothing Stalin ever did during the war led Roosevelt to take a disapproving or critical stance with the single exception of the Berne incident when Stalin harshly accused Roosevelt as well as Churchill of conspiring with the Germans for a selective peace. But FDR never hesitated from the beginning to let his disapproval of imperialism reach Churchill directly.

At the Third Moscow Conference in late 1944, which Roosevelt did not attend, having sent Harriman in his place, Churchill arranged his "percentages" agreement at a private meeting with Stalin that created percentages of Allied versus Russian influence in the several Balkan states. What Churchill wanted was controlling power in Greece, and for this he was willing to concede equally to Stalin influence in other states in the region.

Churchill's reason for wanting control of Greece lay simply in the fact that Communist guerillas, the notorious ELAM and ELAS, were seeking with a great deal of strength to overthrow and take control of the Greek government, which was a very weak and unsettled government in late 1944, requiring Churchill and other ranking British presences to take charge. Had Greece fallen to the Communist guerrillas, the Soviet Union

would quickly have controlled the whole vital eastern end of the Mediterranean, soon perhaps the entire sea.

Roosevelt was angry when he learned from Harriman of the "percentages" agreement, and his anger became fury when Churchill, Eden, and
others went to Greece at Christmas time to assume *de facto* leadership of
the Greek government and its military forces. He instructed Admiral
King to order all American naval forces in the Mediterranean to maintain
a full hygienic distance from such imperialist behavior, even from the
conveying of food and medical supplies to the Greek government.

Britain in Greece at the end of 1944 bothered Roosevelt much more
than did the Soviet violations a few months later of Yalta promises for
Poland and the rest of eastern Europe. While FDR was refusing Churchill's requests for direct action to halt Stalin's terror in Poland, the President
was suggesting that Churchill give his approval to Roosevelt's idea of
sending a high-level international commission into—*not* Poland where
one was desperately needed but—Greece, to perhaps take the sting from
British activities in Greece the preceding Christmas. It would be nice,
Roosevelt suggested, to have the Soviet Commissioner of Trade, Mik-
oyan, on the high-level commission to join in "advising" the Greek
government on its state of economy. Churchill, needless to say, declined
the honor. Ten days passed before he could bring himself to the answer,
which was in the negative and included the following sentence: "We
cannot expect any help from the Russians in the economic sphere, and to
include them in the mission would be a purely political gesture." But
"political gesture" was precisely what Roosevelt had in mind.

Roosevelt's suspicion and gathering resentment of British imperialism
showed itself early in the war in the correspondence. On July 14, 1941,
months before America would even enter the European war, Roosevelt felt it necessary to lecture Churchill, albeit tactfully, even semi-
apologetically. "I know," FDR wrote Churchill, "you will not mind my
mentioning to you a matter which might cause repercussions over here
later on. I refer to rumors which of course are nothing more nor less than
rumors regarding trades or deals which the British government is
alleged to be making with some of the occupied nations." Roosevelt
ended his letter with the words: "I am inclined to think that an overall
statement on your part would be useful at this time, making it clear
that no postwar peace commitments as to territories, populations or econ-
omies have been given. I could then back up your statement in very
strong terms."

Indeed Roosevelt, heir of Woodrow Wilson, could have! When the President had inaugurated the correspondence between the two of them in September 1939, the expressed reason was that of opening a conduit by which the United States might possibly be of help. But "help" had become, by early 1941, with America still months away from active participation in the war, a mini-sermon and righteous warning lest Churchill and England be seen by Americans as thinking in terms of postwar compensation for carrying World War II, the war against Nazism, entirely by herself at that date.

The single most appalling instance of Roosevelt's self-righteousness is undoubtedly that of two years later when he dispatched to Churchill the Hurley report on Iran. Whether or not it was known to the President at the time, Hurley was serving faithfully as an agent for the Sinclair Oil Co. and was actively seeking oil concessions in Iran.[6]

Hurley's report on imperialism and democracy was dispatched by Roosevelt to Churchill with the comment "I rather like his general approach." Given the President's only too well known views on the subject, we may assume that he liked Hurley's "general approach" very much indeed. Wrote Hurley:

We are approaching the irrepressible conflict between worldwide imperialism and worldwide democracy. . . .

What appears to be a new life of British imperialism is the result of the infusion, into its emaciated form, of the blood of productivity and liberty from a free nation through lend lease. British imperialism is being defended today by the blood of the soldiers of the most democratic nation on earth. . . .

It is depressing to note how many of our real friends in the world seem to be irrevocably committed to the old order of imperialism. . . .

We did sustain Britain in the first world war as a first class power but we did not succeed in making the world "safe for democracy." Instead . . . we made the world safe for imperialism. . . .

Britain can be sustained as a first class power but to warrant this support from the American people she must accept the principles of liberty and democracy and discard the principles of oppressive imperialism.

Soviet Russia has earned for herself an assured place as a first class world power. Friendship and cooperation between the United States and the U.S.S.R. are essential to peace and harmony in the post-war world.

Meanwhile Soviet prestige has benefited from their well ordered conduct and by their direct and positive relations with the Iranians.

That Roosevelt would have sent Hurley's "report" to Churchill, as he did on February 29, 1944, with a brief covering letter declaring his general agreement with it, suggests that Hurley's statements—ranging from the fatuous to the aggressively insulting of Great Britain—were prepared explicitly for the precise purpose of being forwarded to Churchill.

Three months passed before Churchill could bring himself to answer, on May 21. "The General . . . makes out . . . that there is an irrepressible conflict between imperialism and democracy. I make bold however to suggest that British imperialism has spread, and is spreading, democracy more widely than any other system of government since the beginning of time." Churchill might have added: "Infinitely more than the social-ist Soviet Union ever has or is likely to in the future." But Roosevelt doubtless would only have chuckled and sent Churchill's reply off to Stalin for enjoyment. Stalin would also have enjoyed Hurley's highly complimentary words on the Soviet Union and its exemplary behavior in Iran.

India was Roosevelt's most consuming obsession. From the correspon-dence between Roosevelt and Churchill one might conclude that second only to the defeat of Germany, the independence of India from the British Empire was Roosevelt's fondest aspiration. His ignorance of the real problems and issues in India was gargantuan. On March 10, 1942—in the same month, be it remembered, in which Roosevelt assured Churchill that Stalin liked and trusted him and that he could "handle" Stalin—Roosevelt out of the blue wrote Churchill that he had given much thought to the "problem" of India and believed "the injection of a new thought" might help resolve the problem.

What was the "new thought"? Precisely this: that India was in the same position the United States had been in during the American Revolution and ripe therefore for a charter akin to the American Articles of Confeder-ation, which would evolve quickly into a second Constitution of the United States.

> Such a move is strictly in line with world changes of the past half century and with *the democratic processes of all who are fighting Nazism*.
>
> I hope that whatever you do the move will be made from London and that there should be no criticism in India that it is being made grudgingly or by compulsion. (Italics added.)

All who are fighting Nazism? The Soviet Union? Democratic processes? By implication in Roosevelt's words to Churchill, the Soviet Union is a part of these "democratic processes," while Britain's custody of India is not.

In his war memoirs, Churchill, after citing the President's letter to him on the problem of India, wrote: "This document is of high interest because it illustrates the difficulties of comparing situations in various countries and scenes where almost every material fact is totally different and the dangers of trying to apply any superficial resemblances which may be noted to the conduct of the war."[7]

"Superficial resemblances" is being charitable to Roosevelt and his gratuitous "injection of a new thought" in the likening, in any degree or for whatever purpose, of the problems of the thirteen American colonies and those of the vast and infinitely diverse peoples of India. To think of the violence that did attend the British relinquishment of sovereignty is to make the President's "new thought" on how to deal with India a mixture of farce and tragedy. As we have seen, Roosevelt was wholly confident and carefree as he doled out pieces of Asia to Stalin at Yalta in return for Stalin's word that the Soviets would join the Pacific war after Hitler was defeated. And once, earlier, in Churchill's hearing, Roosevelt had said to Stalin that America and the Soviets "must meet" sometime to deal with Hong Kong.

On July 29, 1942, only a few months after his "new thought" letter to Churchill, Roosevelt wrote again to push his case for an immediate grant of independence to India by Britain. This time he enclosed a report that he had asked Chiang Kai-shek to prepare on the subject. Chiang Kai-shek on top of General Hurley! Chiang concluded his report: "I earnestly hope the United States would advise both Britain and India in the name of justice and righteousness to seek a reasonable and satisfactory solution for this affects vitally the welfare of mankind. . . . The United States, as the acknowledged leader of democracy, has a natural and vital role to play in bringing about a successful solution of the problem."

That Roosevelt would have sent to Churchill a message such as Chiang's in the still dark days of mid-1942, in as much fundamental ignorance of the realities of India as Chiang himself, or his writers, has to be one of the wonders of the war. One likes to think of the shock, resentment, incredulity, and outrage in Roosevelt had Churchill called the President's attention to the "Negro problem" in the United States and the great advantages to world democracy and a quick winning of the war of an ending of Negro segregation, poverty, and second-class citizenship.

In an answering communication the very next day, July 30, 1942, Churchill made sharply clear the enormous differences between the position of India—divided by caste, race, nationality, religion, and heritage to a degree unmatched anywhere else in the world—and the infant United States. "The Congress Party in no way represents India and is strongly opposed by over ninety million Mohammedans, forty million Untouchables, and the Indian States comprising some ninety millions to whom we are bound by treaty. Congress represents mainly the intelligentsia of non-fighting Hindu elements and can neither defend India nor raise revolt. The military classes on whom everything depends, are thoroughly loyal, in fact over a million have volunteered for the Army. . . . The loyalty would be greatly impaired by handing over the government of India to Congress control. The reckless declarations of Congress have moreover given rise to widespread misgiving, even among its own rank and file."

There is no evidence that such clarification had the slightest effect upon either Roosevelt's or any other American liberal's fixed belief that Great Britain would somehow profit in its desperate war effort by turning all India over immediately to the Congress Party—no party at all in the American and British senses. He seems to have persisted to the end in believing in his "new thought" that India was deep down colonial America. So, doubtless, did he persist to the end in believing that his "plan," which he dispatched in April 1942 by Marshall and Hopkins to the British, to create an almost immediate second front on the Channel would have won the war there and then.

The Cold War began at the Teheran Conference at the end of November 1943. It began with Stalin's unmistakable and unavoidable perception of a fatal flaw in the American-British alliance, the flaw being chiefly President Roosevelt's ineradicable hatred of all imperialism and particularly British imperialism. Stalin's perception included also the fact—how could it not have?—that Roosevelt was eager to curry favor with him, Stalin, and wouldn't hesitate to join him faithfully at the conference table at the expense of Churchill and Britain.

Teheran's significance to the Cold War is much the same that Munich's had been to the beginning of World War II, when Hitler saw the pathetic state of Anglo-French relationships, as manifested by Chamberlain and

Daladier, and the willingness of both to accept almost any condition as an alternative to war.

Teheran was Stalin's Munich, as Munich may be described as Hitler's Teheran. When Stalin learned definitely in his private meetings with Roosevelt that America would not resist Soviet annexations of most of eastern Europe, including Poland, and that the President's chief desire was, along with the defeat of Hitler, to work closely with him both during and after the war, at the expense of British and French imperialistic interests when necessary, toward the eradication of old-fashioned imperialism in the world, the Cold War may be said to have begun. The Cold War, then, began as a Soviet effort to take insidious advantage of American friendship.

Why, it may be asked, should Stalin wish to conduct a war of any kind against so credulous and endlessly generous an ally? First, because he knew that Roosevelt's days on earth were numbered and that his successor was almost certain to be of different clay. Second—and this is the message such wise and experienced minds as Harriman and Kennan tried so hard to convey to Roosevelt, and then Truman—Stalin's Russia was by religio-ideology sworn to destroy capitalism in any shape, form, or fashion, and found it irresistible to open unlocked doors and pillage what was behind them. Only a genuine show of force ever deterred the Soviets. Churchill knew this; Harriman knew it; Kennan and perhaps in less degree Bohlen knew it. But Roosevelt never did learn it. Nor, alas, did his top generals. Marshall, Eisenhower, and a few other high-ranking American military commanders were so dazzled by the Russian generals with whom they joyously fraternized as soon as Germany had surrendered, so persuaded of Russian friendliness toward Uncle Sam, that they were nearly blind to the fact that these happy-go-lucky, friendly, high-ranking Russian officers had not one thing to do with Russian policy in any area. Only the Communist Party had that power, and the Communist Party leadership in 1945 was united in its conviction that war, preferably cold but hot when absolutely necessary, was the bounden duty of Marxist-Leninists in command of powerful Russia. These were matters on which American military minds—not all of them by any means but certainly Marshall, Eisenhower, Eaker, and Bradley—were blissfully ignorant and indifferent; and in surprising measure they remained that way even after 1947. "Like General Marshall," Harriman wrote after the war, "Eisenhower was slow to understand the crucial importance of the Communist Party."[8]

To return to the Teheran conference and Stalin's assessment of what the true relationship was between Churchill and Roosevelt, Britain and America: henceforth the war would be triangular, as Harriman later described it. War between the Allies and Germany, yes; but now a war too between Russia and her western Allies, a covert but not the less determined war.

Russia would conduct and prosecute this war in two or three ways which were clear to Harriman and Churchill among others but never to Roosevelt. The Soviets began methodically in 1944 to subjugate governments of bordering states such as the Baltics, Rumania, Bulgaria, and Jugoslavia, and to threaten Poland in the summer of 1944. Second, and this too was the subject of cables from both Harriman and General Deane in Moscow, the kind of lend-lease supplies the Soviets were increasingly insisting upon—such as whole plants for a given commodity—were clearly not for the war against Germany. Russia was now using lend-lease as the means of achieving postwar superiority in its relations with the West. But Harriman's and Deane's warnings about this were ignored, if they were even read, in the White House.

Something else Stalin became aware of at Teheran was the ease with which he could divide the President and the Prime Minister. Roosevelt's total flip flop on the British Mediterranean Strategy, took place at the Teheran conference in the minute or two it took Stalin to declare his own preference for the Channel assault, with a diversion of troops from the Italian campaign to a landing in southern France. Roosevelt had confirmed his personal acceptance of the Italian campaign and the Mediterranean strategy generally at the Cairo Conference with Churchill and Chiang Kai-shek on the way to Teheran. In an instant at Teheran he retracted that acceptance.

When Stalin taunted Churchill at Teheran about the latter's great enthusiasm for the war against the Bolshevik government back in 1919 and his seeming reluctance to have a second front across the Channel, Roosevelt laughed. So did he when Stalin shocked Churchill with his plan to execute 50,000 German officers at the end of the war. Roosevelt laughed and then participated in the incident. And it is easy to guess at how delighted Stalin was when Roosevelt, in an elaborate and unfunny piece of horseplay just before one of the Conference sessions opened, plainly humiliated Churchill with his teasing about Churchill's resemblance to John Bull. No wonder, as a proud Roosevelt told Frances Perkins when he got back to the White House, Stalin guffawed and also gave a grateful Roosevelt the privilege of calling him "Uncle Joe." There were really all sorts of aspects of that Roosevelt performance at which to laugh and at the same time calculate for the future.

In a way, it is unfair to lash Roosevelt alone for his steadfast, stubborn inability to appreciate the real nature of the Soviets and the totalitarian threat they necessarily posed to the world, to free and democratic governments everywhere. For his own credulity and naiveté were much of America's also, including academic and intellectual America foremost. The concept of totalitarianism and its roots in socialism, populism, nationalism, and the whole idea of "redemptive revolution" in a state were not well known. There were a few who in speech and writing made evident their own insight in this respect: Senator Robert Taft, for one, James Burnham for another. But on the whole, and this was especially true of the liberal mind, the concept of totalitarianism did not strike a knowledgeable response. Better to think of Germany and Italy as reactionary, quintessentially capitalist states called Fascist, and the Soviet Union as being the ultimate contrast with Fascism in its declared socialism.

In Europe, however, as early as the late 1930s there were minds capable of understanding, and writing about, the structural similarity of Communist Russia and Nazi Germany and, in less degree, Fascist Italy. Ortega y Gasset, Emil Lederer, Christopher Dawson, Hermann Rauschning, Peter Drucker, all, before the war broke out, were on record with perceptions of the fact of the overriding *genus totalitarian* within which states as ideologically different as the Soviet Union, Hitler's Germany, and Mussolini's Italy could be properly fitted. A great many American academic writers maintained their stout conviction of the contrary until well after the war, down to the publication of Hannah Arendt's great study of totalitarianism.

But if the President is to be forgiven for sharing an American intellectual incapability of recognizing the totalitarian phenomenon and thus the centrality of the totalitarian war on democracy, we should remember that he received on-the-site advice, often frantic advice, from his own trusted aides, Harriman perhaps foremost among them, about Soviet depredations upon eastern Europe and Soviet malfeasances with respect to American lend-lease. As we have seen, Churchill wrote tirelessly through the months immediately following Yalta, as did Harriman and Deane, trying to convince Roosevelt of what their own eyes and intelligence told them was going on. It was futile. He was still forgiving Stalin when he died.

Churchill has been accused of lacking any real sense of Russia as a totalitarian state, in contrast to a mere dictatorship. But the instantaneous vehemence of his personal war on the new Bolshevik regime when it came into existence in late 1917 and his relentless campaign after the war to alert Europe to the danger of Soviet socialist internationalism suggest a mind well beyond Roosevelt's in understanding.

Churchill agreed in 1939, before the war had broken out, to a publisher's request to write a book on the subject of Europe since the Russian Revolution. One's mouth can water at the thought of such a book. But late in the war Churchill informed his publisher that the book was not to be. To write the kind of book he had had in mind back in 1939 was no longer possible for him.

"If we win the war it will be followed by a peace conference. If I am still Prime Minister, I shall be a member of that peace conference. I could not write about any of these countries and give a critical and unbiased description of how they behaved in the intervening years, because it would hamper any possibility of amicable agreements." Churchill added: "Good arrangements will have to be made. I could not fling out a lot of interesting but essential matter from the old quarrels that have passed, and build upon situations which no longer exist. I certainly should not be on speaking terms with Stalin if I wrote the things I would have in time of peace. To ask me to do this, is a thing that no reasonable person would do. . . . Am I to bring up the horrors of the Russian Revolution? My whole outlook is changed. The synopsis which was a living thing then [in 1939] is now dead. Twenty Years Alliance with Russia."[9]

Churchill was writing as a Prime Minister who hoped to remain Prime Minister when the peace conference began. That is not only understandable, it is, all things considered, laudable. We are still entitled, though, to sigh at the loss of what might well have become a classic had he chosen to yield it in the years between his Prime Ministerships. We can fairly guess what his overarching perspective would have been. As is evident from recorded remarks he made to close, trusted intimates, throughout the war, his fear of the postwar Soviet Union was at least as great as had been his fear of Nazi Germany from 1933 on.

In Sir John Colville's *Diaries* there is an entry that confirms the somberness of Churchill's mind about the Soviet-Europe future. At a small dinner one night Churchill expounded his pessimism. "Chamberlain had trusted Hitler as he was trusting Stalin though he thought there were differences of circumstances between the two." The next night, at the same table, Churchill continued his mood of melancholy. "What will lie between the white snows of Russia and the white cliffs of Dover? Perhaps however the Russians would not want to sweep to the Atlantic or something might stop them as the accident of Genghis Khan's death had stopped the horsed archers of the Mongols who retired and never came back."[10] At Quebec, as I have noted, Churchill told his physician that he saw "bloody consequences" in the future, adding that "Stalin is an unnatural man." And, as we have also seen, he wrote at Eden's request his views on the postwar situation in Europe in which he stressed the importance of the European countries forming a United States of Europe from which the Soviets would be excluded and through which a containment of Soviet Communist aggression could be effected. And there was, shortly after the war, the famous Iron Curtain address he made in Fulton, Missouri, at President Truman's request. Churchill had used that now historic phrase once before, in a telegram.

There is simply nothing comparable to be found in Roosevelt's thinking about Stalin and the Soviets; nothing remotely comparable. There is only the vivid, unvarnishable fact that under his Wilsonian philosophy of world history, Roosevelt saw British imperialism as Wilson had seen it a quarter century earlier, as a greater danger to democracy than the Soviet Union, Stalin included. So great was Roosevelt's confidence that he could "personally handle" Stalin, now and later, that he was willing even to suffer rebuffs and insults from Stalin, to go out of his way occasionally to put Churchill down in Stalin's presence, in order to be certain that he and Stalin would work together at the very top of the United Nations to reconstruct the world, to bring democracy and liberty to peoples everywhere.

Puerility, in Kennan's wording, it assuredly was. But it was an episode of political romanticism and misguided moralism that America would suffer from for close to a half-century after FDR's death at Warm Springs. There were statesmen, including Hull, Harriman, Kelley, Henderson, Kennan, Bohlen, and Bullitt, among others, perfectly qualified to have given FDR some of the most expert and dispassionate advice to be had in the world on the Soviets. Only once did Roosevelt allow Hull to attend any of the international summit conferences. But from late 1941 on, when Roosevelt and Hopkins were working frenetically for as much centralization of lend-lease as possible in the White House, in order to expedite shipments to Stalin, none of the experts and wise men on the Soviets were welcome when and if they brought bad tidings on Soviet behavior in Poland or elsewhere. Nor were most of these men permitted to be present at Yalta in February 1945.

Truman changed all this measurably. For the first time, the voices of

Harriman, Kennan, Bohlen, and the others, could be heard in the White House; others like Lovett, Forrestal, McCloy, of often like sentiments, could be heard also. But not even Truman could rout altogether the pro-Roosevelt, pro-Soviet following in America. Thus in 1948 the so-called Independent Progressive Party, nominated Henry Wallace—whom Truman had fired for disloyalty—as a Communist figurehead candidate for President. The real direction of the Party was in the hands of several Communists and several more devoted fellow-travellers. The sole purpose of Wallace's candidacy was the destruction of Truman's presidency— which was targeted because of Truman's sharp turn against FDR's policy of Soviet courtship.

The ridiculous Independent Progressive Party was virtually forgotten within a couple of years. But the underlying principle of the Party—that the Soviet Union is basically a forward-looking, progressive state seeking a prosperous, democratic, and classless society not unlike that struggled for by William Jennings Bryan, Woodrow Wilson, and Franklin D. Roosevelt—has by no means disappeared. There is still today a substantial sector of the American intelligentsia, one with considerable influence upon some of our otherwise excellent newspapers and broadcast news agencies, that comes very close at times to holding precisely that view.

There is little doubt that Roosevelt was impressed by Stalin's power, personal power, used, as he saw it, in behalf of the Soviet people. Roosevelt loved personal power, perhaps more than any other American President. His original NRA, soon ruled unconstitutional by the Supreme Court, gave him great and sweeping powers which Congress could not have trimmed. In his pique at the Court's outlawing of the NRA, Roosevelt thought up the Court-packing bill, one that would have allowed him to appoint half a dozen new justices, all suitably principled, of course, so that he could rule without interference from the Court. He seems to have been contemptuous of Churchill's obligation to report regularly during the war to the War Cabinet and to be ready at a moment's notice to go before the House of Commons and explain and defend his direction of government and war. Roosevelt had no such obligation and therefore no such inclination. Churchill once, while standing between Stalin and Roosevelt, said: "Here am I, instrument of democracy, standing between two dictators."

Once Roosevelt mused aloud: "Woodrow Wilson said we are making the world safe for democracy; but can democracy make the world safe for it?"[11] A nice question indeed. So must have Julius Caesar and then Augustus Caesar wondered as they sought to "save" the Roman Republic.

Napoleon declared his mission was saving the French Republic. The idea of the People represented by the One, whose dedication to his constituency is supreme in his mind and who, like Rousseau's Legislator, radiates only the power of the People, is one of the most tantalizing ideas to be found in all the history of political power. Nothing that had happened to Franklin Delano Roosevelt ever lessened his passion for power. When he returned from Yalta to go before Congress and report triumph, he said he had found it easy to work with Mr. Stalin "who is a realist, like me."

Roosevelt left a double legacy. Ironically each legacy had failed in its stated purpose. The New Deal is the first of the two legacies. It not only failed to end or significantly affect the Depression, it was less successful economically than either England's or Germany's responses during the 1930s. Yet the New Deal not only survived; it prospered in the form of a welfare state. To this day, the American welfare state is intrinsically no more than the New Deal enlarged.

The second legacy from Roosevelt is rooted in his courtship of Stalin during World War II. That courtship failed abysmally. Designed to employ the arts of seduction upon an eastern despot in order to convert him into an FDR democrat, the courtship not only yielded Roosevelt insults from Stalin throughout the war, it blew up in his face, in Poland, Rumania, the Baltic States, and elsewhere as Roosevelt was dying in Warm Springs. By the end of 1945, certainly by early 1946, it was apparent to the world that Stalin was occupying nations ruthlessly and subjecting their governments to constant terror. Within six months after VJ Day, Stalin's totalitarian Russia was astride the Eurasian Heartland. It was only the still exclusive possession of the nuclear bomb in America's hands that forced Stalin to drop any ideas he had about sending the Red Army into devastated western Europe in late 1945.

Roosevelt's plan for seducing Stalin and turning the Soviet Union toward the cause of world peace and democracy failed, but that did not prevent the plan from entering the hearts and minds of millions of Americans, overwhelmingly liberal progressives, most of them from the universities, the main line churches, and the entertainment industry. They have found it possible during most of the postwar period to harbor the same illusions respecting the Soviets that Roosevelt persisted in to the moment of his death. Roosevelt thought that Stalin's Russia was to be preferred as a partner of the U.S. in the postwar world to either Great Britain or any of the rest of the world's states which could be labeled "imperialist," "reactionary," and "corrupt." As Jeane Kirkpatrick wrote a decade ago in her now historic essay, "Dictatorships and Double Standards," a large body of American thought, mostly liberal-progressive, has held the identical view for the past forty and more years. Why have so many American intellectuals held to this perspective? Because, Ambassador Kirkpatrick writes, "some modern Americans prefer 'socialist' to traditional autocracies." Their basic reason for this preference is that socialism, no matter how despotic it may seem at times, is nevertheless "modern." It is modern in that it falls, albeit perversely at times, in the whole rationalist-utilitarian vein of thought that was born of the Enlightenment and that, in somewhat different forms, contains liberalism and social democracy, above all, egalitarianism.

"Traditional autocracies," writes Kirkpatrick, "are, in general and in their very nature, deeply offensive to modern American sensibilities. The notion that public affairs should be ordered on the basis of kinship, friendship and other personal relations rather than on the basis of objective 'rational' standards violates our conception of justice and efficiency."[12]

This, as Jeane Kirkpatrick demonstrates at length, is the source of the double standard that so many liberal minds have applied to the world's powers. To the liberal-progressive there is something inherently, ineradicably, more shameful, more corrupting and despotic, in a Diem South Viet Nam, a Marcos Philippines, or a Boer South Africa than in a Marxist-Leninist Soviet Union, even a Stalinist Soviet Union. Even during the height of Stalinist terror and butchery, the Western, and especially American, liberal, infatuated with his scheme of human progress, steadfastly maintained that Russia was at bottom a freer, more equal and just state than that which had existed under the czars. The same underlying dogma of progress underlies the preference for Castro over Batista, Ho Chi Minh over Diem, and the Sandinistas over the Somozas. And, within this historical perspective, this allegedly "objective" vision of the world, contemporary South Africa is immeasurably more despotic, more a terrorist state, than Soviet Russia was at the height of Stalinism. For, the reasoning goes, underneath even the worst of the Great Terror in the Soviet Union, there lay a "modern," "rational," "progressive" socialism that would shortly shed its purely coincidental totalitarianism.

Thus the farce that began on March 18, 1942, when Roosevelt assured Churchill that he could personally handle Stalin went on for more than forty years in a considerable part of the American mind. Whether the farce has even yet ended only the imminent future will tell.

NOTES
AND
REFERENCES

INTRODUCTION

1. Frances Perkins, *The Roosevelt I Knew.* New York, 1946, pp. 86–87.
2. Averell Harriman, *Special Envoy to Churchill and Stalin.* New York, 1975, p. 170.
3. Harriman, p. 444.
4. George Kennan, *Russia and the West Under Lenin and Stalin.* Boston, 1960, p. 355.
5. *For the President: Personal and Secret: Correspondence Between Franklin D. Roosevelt and William C. Bullitt.* Edited by Orville E. Bullitt. Boston, 1972. Bullitt's letter is dated January 29, 1943. Kennan's praise is in his Introduction.
6. "How We Won the War and Lost the Peace." *Life,* August 30, 1948. The editor notes on page 554 of the Bullitt Correspondence that an almost identical rendering of the President's words is to be found in a book by a visiting French journalist, Laslo Havas, *Assassinat au Sommet.*
7. *Churchill and Roosevelt: The Complete Correspondence.* Edited by Warren Kimball. Princeton, 1984, 3 vols, vol. 1, p. 5.
8. John Colville, *The Fringes of Power: 10 Downing Street: Diaries, 1939–1955.* New York, 1985, p. 624.
9. Martin Gilbert, *Winston S. Churchill: Road to Victory 1941–1945.* Boston, 1986, pp. 239–240.
10. Cited by Vojtech Mastny, *Russia's Road to the Cold War.* New York, 1979, p. 108. I thank Paul Seabury for this reference.
11. Harriman, p. 226. Gilbert, p. 482.

111

CHAPTER ONE

1. *Correspondence.* Roosevelt to Churchill, March 18, 1942. Hereafter references to the correspondence exchanged between Roosevelt and Churchill will be confined to dates of the messages given in the text. Letters and telegrams are arranged chronologically.
2. George Kennan, *Memoirs: 1925–1950.* New York, 1967, pp. 84–85.
3. Walter Isaacson and Evan Thomas, *The Wise Men.* New York, 1986, p. 225.
4. Raymond J. Sontag. *Nazi-Soviet Documents, 1939–1941.* Washington, D.C., p. 340 f.
5. Kennan, *Russia and the West,* p. 352.
6. Kennan, *Russia and the West,* p. 353.
7. Robert Sherwood, *Roosevelt and Hopkins.* New York, 1948, p. 2.
8. Cited in Robert Dallek, *Franklin D. Roosevelt and American Foreign Policy, 1932–1945.* New York, 1979, pp. 279–280.
9. Sherwood, p. 322.
10. Sherwood, Chapter 15, *passim.*
11. Raymond H. Dawson, *The Decision to Aid Russia, 1941.* Chapel Hill, 1959, p. 117.
12. Dawson, p. 156.
13. Dawson, p. 152.
14. Dawson, p. 256.
15. Dawson, p. 104.
16. Dawson, p. 235.
17. Dawson, p. 259.
18. Dallek, pp. 298 and 521.
19. Dawson, p. 211.
20. Gilbert, p. 99.
21. Gilbert, p. 106.
22. Harriman, p. 157, and Gilbert p. 183 f.
23. Kimball, *Correspondence,* I, p. 616.
24. Gilbert, p. 90 f.
25. Mark A. Stoler, *The Politics of the Second Front.* New York, 1977, p. 42.
26. Stoler, p. 42. The excerpt from Hopkins is in Sherwood, p. 526.
27. Gilbert, p. 843.
28. Gilbert, p. 132.
29. Stoler, p. 47.
30. Gilbert, pp. 119–120.
31. Gilbert, pp. 379–380.

CHAPTER TWO

1. *Stalin's Correspondence with Roosevelt and Truman, 1941–1945.* Capricorn Books, New York, 1965, (a publication of the Ministry of Foreign Affairs of the USSR) pp. 22–23.
2. Stalin Correspondence, p. 42.
3. Stalin Correspondence, p. 44.
4. Stalin Correspondence, p. 50.

5. Elliot Roosevelt, *As He Saw It,* New York, 1946, p. 117.
6. Sherwood, p. 696.
7. Gilbert, p. 581.
8. Roosevelt was stung when he learned of Stalin's judgment on unconditional surrender, and professed not to have heard the Marshal at Teheran. In the *Correspondence,* II, page 645, there is a letter from Churchill to FDR impressing upon him that he had indeed heard Stalin so declare himself.
9. Harriman, p. 264; Gilbert, pp. 568–9.
10. A transcript of private as well as public meetings at Teheran is contained in the Cairo and Teheran volume of the *Foreign Relations of the United States* series (hereafter referred to as *FRUS*), published by the Department of State. The three private conversations are found on pages 483–486, 529–533, and 594–596. I see no point in going beyond this reference in my treatment in the text of the conversations.
11. A.J.P. Taylor, *Beaverbrook.* London, 1972, p. 397.
12. Dallek, pp. 436–437.
13. Charles E. Bohlen, *Witness to History.* New York, 1973. pp. 141 and 146.
14. Perkins, p. 84.
15. Keith Eubank, *Summit at Teheran.* New York, 1985, p. 351.
16. Sir Alexander Cadogan. *Diaries.* New York, 1972, p. 581.
17. Cadogan, p. 582.
18. Eubank, p. 311.
19. Isaacson and Thomas, pp. 260–261.
20. Sir John Wheeler-Bennett. *The Semblance of Peace.* London, 1972, p. 290.
21. *FRUS,* p. 553.
22. *FRUS,* p. 553 f. See Gilbert, p. 580.
23. Gilbert, p. 581.
24. *FRUS,* p. 112.
25. *FRUS,* pp. 128–129.
26. Churchill to Roosevelt, March 3, 1944.
27. Churchill to Roosevelt, March 3 and March 4, 1944.
28. Gilbert, pp. 961–962.
29. Isaacson and Thomas, p. 238.
30. Gilbert, p. 870.
31. Kennan, *Russia and the West,* p. 357.
32. Gilbert, p. 949.
33. Gilbert, p. 760.
34. Gilbert, pp. 548–549.
35. FRUS, Cairo-Teheran, p. 359; Gilbert, p. 565.
36. Gilbert, p. 558.
37. *FRUS,* pp. 494–495.
38. *FRUS,* p. 495.
39. Stoler, p. 148.
40. Stoler, pp. 145–148; Cadogan, p. 582.
41. Kimball, *Correspondence,* III, 288.

42. Sir Arthur Bryant, *Triumph in the West: Based on the Diaries of Lord Alanbrooke.* New York, 1959, p. 168.
43. Mark Clark, *Calculated Risk.* New York, 1950, p. 368 f.
44. Gilbert, p. 1325.

CHAPTER THREE

1. Forrest C. Pogue, *George Marshall,* vol. 3, New York, 1973, p. 528.
2. Chester Wilmot, *The Struggle for Europe.* New York, 1953, p. 654.
3. *New York Review of Books,* June 11, 1987, p. 50.
4. *FRUS,* Malta and Yalta, pp. 727–728.
5. Bryant-Alanbrooke, p. 304.
6. *FRUS,* Yalta, p. 572.
7. *FRUS,* Yalta, p. 618 et seq.
8. *FRUS,* Yalta, p. 618 et seq.
9. Gilbert, p. 1265.
10. *FRUS,* Yalta, pp. 766–771, furnishes the full and official transcript of the Roosevelt-Stalin meeting on Asia.
11. Sherwood, p. 867.
12. Harriman, p. 399.
13. Stalin Correspondence, pp. 211–12.
14. This and other cables by Harriman to the President, along with alarms and warnings also by Kennan and Bohlen can be found in Isaacson and Thomas, pp. 225-290 and Harriman, pages 418–446. In his diary, Harriman lamented that "the President consistently shows very little interest in Eastern European countries except as they affect sentiment in America."
15. Harriman, pp. 437–438.
16. Roosevelt's drafted, and duly dispatched, reply to Stalin is in vol. III, p. 612 of the *Correspondence.* Stalin's letters to Roosevelt and Stalin, including his curt, contemptuous reply to Roosevelt's explanation of the Berne incident, are in *Stalin's Correspondence,* pp. 205–208.
17. Isaacson and Thomas, p. 247 f.
18. Harriman, p. 422.
19. Harriman, p. 423.
20. Wheeler-Bennett, p. 298.
21. Harriman, p. 444.
22. Kimball, *Correspondence,* III, p. 617.
23. Kimball, *Correspondence,* III, April 11, Harriman, pp. 439–440. *Stalin's Correspondence,* p. 214.
24. *FRUS,* Malta and Yalta, pp. 570–571.
25. Gilbert, pp. 1273–1275.
26. Nigel Hamilton, *Monty: The Field Marshall 1944–1946.* London, 1986, p. 480.

CHAPTER FOUR

1. Wheeler-Bennett, p. 8.
2. Edward R. Stettinius, *Diaries,* New York, 1975, p. 40.
3. Wilmot, p. 695.

4. Gilbert, p. 15.

5. Bryant, p. 64.

6. Kimball, editorial commentary in *Correspondence,* vol III, p. 3. The paragraphs following are all from Hurley's report to the President, a copy of which Roosevelt sent to Churchill for his consideration along with a letter dated February 29, 1944.

7. Churchill, *History of the Second World War.* New York, vol. 4, p. 213.

8. Isaacson and Thomas, p. 318.

9. Gilbert, pp. 949–950.

10. Colville, pp. 562–563.

11. Dallek, p. 606 n.

12. Jeane Kirkpatrick, *Dictatorships and Double Standards.* New York, 1982, pp. 44–45.

INDEX

117